D1359042

Vest Pocket
JAPANESE

TITLES IN THIS SERIES

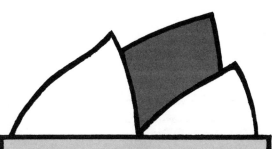

Vest Pocket
JAPANESE

Formerly published as: JAPANESE IN A NUTSHELL

By
TAKESHI HATTORI, Litt.D.
Professor
Hokkaido Gakugei University
and
WAKAKO YOKOO, M.A.
Columbia University
Lecturer in English
Aoyama Gakuin University

PUBLISHED BY

INSTITUTE FOR LANGUAGE STUDY
Westport, Connecticut 06880

DISTRIBUTED TO THE BOOK TRADE BY
HENRY HOLT & COMPANY

Library of Congress Cataloging-in-Publication Data

Hattori, Takeshi, 1909–
    Vest Pocket Japanese.

    Previously published as: Japanese in a Nutshell.
    1. Japanese language—Conversation and phrase books
—English. 2. Japanese language—Grammar—1950–
3. Japanese language—Dictionaries—English. 4. English
language—Dictionaries—Japanese. I. Yokoo, Wakako.
II. Title.
PL539.H39 1989   495.6'83421   89–15384
ISBN 0–8489–5108–5

First Edition

Copyright © 1967 Institute for Language Study

All Rights Reserved

Printed in the United States of America

HH Editions 9 8 7 6 5 4 3   0008-5

HOW TO USE THIS BOOK

From cuisine to cameras, Japan has exerted tremendous influence upon the American market. Not only are trade relations growing with this Far Eastern country, but also there has been a marked increase in American-Japanese cultural exchange. In order to improve our understanding and appreciation of this fascinating Oriental people and their culture, a knowledge of the language which expresses the unique and unusual aspects of the Japanese character is essential.

The purpose of this text is to introduce modern conversational Japanese to the English speaker who has not necessarily had any prior language-learning experience. As Japanese is not a member of the same language family as is English, the authors of this book have tried to present it in the clearest possible way. With practice and a desire to learn, the student will encounter no difficulty in mastering conversational Japanese—both spoken and written.

Years of research and experience have helped to make this book unique; some of its special features are outlined below:

In the KEY TO PRONUNCIATION, each sound is explained, with special attention given to more difficult sounds so that the student may acquire correct pronunciation habits. The Japanese system of writing is a combination of Chinese and KANA characters. KANA characters are phonetic symbols for grammatical and stylistic elements which are peculiar to the Japanese language. Thus it is important to know KANA in order to master Japanese vocabulary, grammar and pronunciation. One of the unique features of this book is the systematic presentation of KANA in the syllabary (table of syllables). The KANA characters are also given in ROMAJI—the Romanized spelling of Japanese.

The BASIC SENTENCE PATTERNS cover the basic structure of Japanese sentences so that the student readily understands the fundamentals of the language without being unnecessarily burdened with constructions that are used rarely.

1

The EVERYDAY CONVERSATIONS deal with daily situations which the visitor to Japan is likely to encounter. Cultural footnotes and explanations enable the student to learn about Japan and its people, as well as how to speak, read and write its language. This, coupled with illustrations animating the text, helps to make learning more enjoyable.

Each of the sentences in the above two sections is given in the Japanese system of writing, Romaji, and then in English translation. The Romaji is aligned with the Japanese, permitting rapid comprehension of the pronunciation of normal Japanese writing. Since the Japanese are just beginning to use western-style punctuation, inconsistencies often occur. Therefore, for easy comparison with the Romaji, we have only used commas and periods in the Japanese writing. In the Romaji, normal punctuation has been used. Whenever necessary, both free and literal English translations are provided.

The OUTLINE OF GRAMMAR incorporates all of the essential grammatical features of Japanese which the student must know, and explains them in terms which he will understand. Special attention is given to those Japanese constructions which do not exist in English.

Finally, there is a JAPANESE-ENGLISH and ENGLISH-JAPANESE DICTIONARY, both sections including almost 5000 entries: all the words used in the EVERYDAY CONVERSATIONS, in addition to words and phrases selected because of their frequent use in modern spoken Japanese. The DICTIONARY lists each entry in three forms: Japanese, Romaji and English, with variants and literal meanings given. In the JAPANESE-ENGLISH section, the entries are arranged according to Romaji or Latin alphabetical order for quick reference.

For those who have not already purchased the recordings, the dialogues of the text have been flawlessly reproduced on records and tapes. The foreign voices are those of professionals who have been selected for their perfect pronunciation and accent, as well as for their pleasant voice quality. Systematic use of these recordings of authentic conversational Japanese will accustom both your ear and tongue to the foreign sounds, and thereby help you develop a real "feeling" for the language. And, by means of frequent repetition and practice, you soon will acquire a proficiency in Japanese that will both amaze and gratify you.

TABLE OF CONTENTS

*Numbers preceding each item refer to paragraph numbers in book.

3

*Numbers preceding each item refer to paragraph numbers in book.

KEY TO PRONUNCIATION

Broadly speaking, the often-repeated statement that in Japanese the consonants are pronounced as in English and the vowels as in Italian is true.

PRONUNCIATION OF THE CONSONANTS

1. All the consonants are pronounced similarly to those of English except the **n** in word-final position, as in **hon** *book*, **bun** *a part*, and the **r**. The consonants are followed either by a vowel or by a vowel plus **n**; consonants other than **n** never appear in word-final position. In the following examples the consonants preceding a vowel will be pronounced without any difficulty.

JAPANESE CONSONANTS	DESCRIPTION	EXAMPLES	
p	As *p* in pill poll	**pedaru*** **pasu***	pedal pass
t	As *t* in ten tool	**taka** **hito**	hawk man
k	As *k* in kill, or *c* in cool Kodak	**kane** **hako**	money box
b	As *b* in bill bale	**beru*** **kabi**	bell mold
d	As *d* in dell doll	**doro** **sode**	mud sleeve
g	As *g* in gill (of a fish) gale; never as in Jill	**giri** **gake**	obligation cliff, precipice
f	As *f* in full, BUT use both lips in pronouncing it, and not upper teeth and lower lip	**futa** **hifu**	lid skin
s	As *s* in sail sole	**sake** **kiso**	rice-wine basis
h	As *h* in hole hill; before Japanese **i, h** may also be articulated as in German *ich*	**hasu** **hima**	lotus time to spare
z	As *z* in zest gauze **z** may also be pronounced as *dz* in adze or as *ds* in cads	**zoku** **mizu**	rebel, thief water

---

* Borrowings from English.

j	As *j* in Jill	**jiku**	axis
	jar; **j** may also be pronounced as *dg* in edge	**haji**	dishonor
m	As *m* in mill	**muda**	no avail
	mull	**yama**	mountain
n	As *n* in nil	**nawa**	rope
	noon	**yani**	resin
	(Note: Further remarks concerning **n**, see p. 10)		
w	As *w* in will	**wata**	cotton wool
	want	**niwa**	garden
y	As *y* in yule	**yado**	inn, hotel
	yawn	**yume**	dream

The consonant **r.** Japanese **r** is completely different from the American "rolled" *r* and even different from the various European varieties of *r* pronounced by flapping or rolling the tip of the tongue against the upper teeth or against the ridge behind them. To approximate Japanese **r,** practice saying the English name *Teddy* by pronouncing the *dd* very briefly and with a minimum of pressure by merely touching the ridge behind the upper teeth with the tip of the tongue. If successful, such practice should result in the Japanese word **teri** which means *shining upon.* At all costs, avoid the American *r.*

Further examples : **furo**   bath
          hiru   daytime
          riku   land   (as opp. to *sea*)
          roku   six

The consonants **ch, sh,** and **ts.** The Japanese do not pronounce **t** and **s** before the vowel **i,** as *t* and *s* in English *tea, sea,* etc.; in Japanese these two consonants are palatalized before **i,** thus, we use the symbols **ch** and **sh** as shown in the following examples :

ch   As *ch* in chill, e. g. **chiri** dust, **uchi** house, inside
sh   As *sh* in sheet, e. g. **shima** island, **ushi** bull

Ch and **sh** also appear before the vowels **a, o** and **u,** as in the examples below :

ch   As *ch* in choice, e. g. **chasaji**   teaspoon
               shichō   mayor
               chūsha   injection

sh	As *sh* in shoe,	e. g.	**shashin**	photography, photo
			shumi	hobby
			shōyu	soy

The consonant **t** does not occur before the vowel **u,** so that in Japanese not **tu,** as in English too, two, etc., but **tsu** is heard. Thus, for this consonant the symbol:

ts	As *ts* in	cats	e. g.	**tsuki**	moon, month
		dots		**satsu**	paper money

N. B. Although **ch, sh** and **ts** are single consonants, the symbols for them are composed of two letters respectively.

REMARKS ON THE CONSONANTS

2. The Double Consonants. When a double consonant occurs in Japanese (**pp, tt, kk, ss, mm, nn**), it must be pronounced doubly long. Thus, the difference in the pronunciation of the long consonant **nn** vs. the short **n** (e. g., **anna,** *such a* vs. **ana,** *hole*) corresponds to a similar difference in English (e.g., Have you seen Ned? vs. Have you seen Ed?). Practice the following pairs: (1) **hatta,** *he pasted it on* vs. **hata,** *flag;* (2) **massao,** *completely blue* vs. **Masao** (boy's name).

Further examples :	**ippai**	a cupful, a glassful
	totte	handle, knob
	shikki	humidity, lacquerware
	amma	masseur, masseuse

Since **ch, sh,** and **ts** are single consonants, they can also occur long. In such cases they are respectively written **tch, ssh** and **tts.**

Examples :	**itchi**	agreement, concurrence
	kitchiri	precisely, punctually
	shittsui	loss
	ittsui	a pair
	isshu	a kind
	isshō	a lifetime

3. The letter *m* before *b* or *p*. In the spelling used in this book (and in many others), **m** is written before **b** and **p,** and **n** before all other consonants. Thus, the word **hon,** *book,* appears as **hom-** in **hombako,** *bookcase,* but as **hon-** in **hondana,** *bookshelf.* The spelling thus reflects a natural alternation in the Japanese language.

4. The word-final *n*. When Japanese **n** appears in word-final position, as in **hon,** *book,* **gohan,** *food, rice,* **bin,** *bottle,* **bun,** *a part,* it is not pronounced as a clear *n* as in English; but, rather, the vowel which precedes it is strongly nasalized, as in French **bon,** *good,* (or more accurately, as in Castilian Spanish **ven,** *come!*).   American speakers who normally have a similar kind of nasal intonation are often said to speak with a "nasal twang".   Try to approximate this "twang" when pronouncing word-final Japanese **n.**—The same applies to Japanese **n** within the word when it appears before **s** (as in **Kansai,** the name of a province south of Tokyo), before **z** (as in **anzen,** *safety*), and before **y** (as in **panya,** *bakery*).

5. The pronunciation of *ni*. When Japanese **n** appears before **i,** it is not pronounced as in English but as in Spanish *ñ* (or French and Italian *gn*), with the middle section of the tongue touching the two extremes of the roof of the mouth. Practice: **kani,** *crab,* **nani,** *what?*

6. The nasalized *g*. In Tokyo and in the areas north of it, Japanese **g** within the word is almost always pronounced as English **ng** in *hanger* (not as in finger [fing-ger]).   Thus, the Japanese word **migi,** *right-hand side,* in Tokyo sounds more like **Ming-EE,** to the English speaker, than like **Mig-EE.**   You may choose either way of pronouncing this **g** within the word.   In previous years, the "Southern" pronunciation (simple **g**) carried more prestige because it was typical of Kyoto, Japan's traditional cultural capital.

7. Alternations of consonants. A number of Japanese consonants alternate with each other in given positions. The following table lists these alternations, but the student is not expected to memorize them, since they are more easily acquired as part of the vocabulary :

THE CONSONANT	ALTERNATES WITH	SINGLE WORD	WHEN REDUPLICATED	OTHER EXAMPLES
f	b	**fushi** joint, knuckle	**fushi-bushi** every joint, all knuckles	**watashi-bune** ferryboat **fune** boat
f	p	**(fun)*** confused	**fun-pun** pell-mell	**yom-pun** four minutes **fun** minute
h	b	**hito** man	**hito-bito** people	**hari-bako** workbox **hako** box
t	d	**toki** time	**toki-doki** sometimes	**hon-dana** bookshelf **tana** shelf
s	z	**sore** that	**sore-zore** each	**hai-zara** ashtray **sara** plate
k	g	**kami** god	**kami-gami** gods	**kawa-gishi** riverbank **kishi** bank, shore
ch	j	**chiru** disperse	**chiri-jiri** dispersedly, helter-skelter	**hana-ji** nosebleed **chi** blood
sh	j	**shima** island	**shima-jima** islands	**ko-jima** small island
ts	z	**tsuki** moon, month	**tsuki-zuki** every month	**ko-zukai** janitor **tsukai** messenger

*Note particularly that this form can be represented in writing only by its Chinese character.

PRONUNCIATION OF THE VOWELS

8. In standard Japanese there are only five vowels, **a, i, u, e, o,** which are pronounced as follows:

a   as in English *par*, but much shorter; thus Japanese **kami,** *paper*, is quite similar to English *Commie* (as pronounced by an American).

i   as in English *peer*, but shorter and with greater stricture (narrowness) in the mouth, as in French or Spanish. Thus, Japanese **mimi,** *ear*, is closer to the French pronunciation of the name **Mimi** than to its English pronunciation.

u   as in English *poor*, but with no rounding of the lips (that is, rather with an exaggerated smile). Thus, the last two syllables of the theatrical genre called **kabuki** sound like English *bookie* said with the corners of the mouth spread far apart.

e   as in English *pear* or *pet*. Japanese **ebi**, *shrimp*, is close to English *Debbie* without the initial *D*. Be absolutely sure to avoid a gliding sound in Japanese word-final **e** (as in **kane**, *money*, **ke**, *hair*); that is, make sure that these words do not end in the English syllables *nay* and *Kay*. The vowel should be abrupt as in the affirmation spelled *yeh* in English.

o   as in English *pour* or *tore*, but much shorter, as in French *pot*, or in Spanish *o*. As in the case of **e,** avoid the gliding sound as it is found in English *so, toe, oh*. Thus, Japanese **oto**, *sound, noise*, should not sound like *oh toe* but rather like the French pronunciation of *auto* or the German vowels in *Otto*.

9. Long Vowels. As in the case of the consonants, vowels marked long (ā, ū, ē, ō) are pronounced doubly long. This also applies to long **i**, written **ii**. Words with long **ā** and **ē** are rare (**okāsan**, *mother*, **onēsan**, *elder sister*). Again, care should be taken not to pronounce the sequence **onē** in the latter as in English *oh nay*. Rather, **ē** should resemble the vowel in English *pear, care, air* (of course, without *r*). Long **ū** should be pronounced "smiling" that is, with the corners of the mouth stretched apart : **shū**, *week*, is similar to English *shoe* but the lip-rounding is absent. The greatest care should be taken not to pronounce Japanese **sō** and English *so* alike, in spite of the fact that they mean the same thing. Japanese **sō** completely lacks the gliding sound of the long **o** in English *so* and should be pronounced more like English *saw* than like English *so*. Practice: **horenso**, *spinach*, avoiding English *hoe-wren-so* and keeping in mind what has been said about **n** before **s** (see 4). The long **i** (written **ii**) is pronounced as in English:

meet, meat, key, pea. Care should be taken to render it long: **torii,** *front gate of a Shinto shrine,* vs. **tori,** *bird.*

10. The combinations of vowels. Combinations of vowels in Japanese (**ai, ei, oi, ui; ou, iu, au**) are pronounced as the sum of their constituent parts. Thus **ai,** *love,* is pronounced as **a-i;** that is, similar to English *eye* (but with a much shorter **a**-sound); **rei,** *example,* as in English *ray* (but with a Japanese **r**—see above 1); **koi,** *carp* as in English *coy* (but with a shorter **o**); **kau,** *to buy,* as in English *cow* (but with a shorter **a**; concerning **u,** see above 8). Some Japanese pronounce **ei** as **ē**; either pronunciation is acceptable.

11. The whispered vowels *u* and *i*. Two short vowels **u** and **i,** are often omitted (or more accurately, are pronounced in a whisper) especially when preceded by **s, h, f, ts,** and **ch.** For example **sukoshi,** *a little,* can be heard as **skoshi, hiku,** *to pull,* as **hku** (where **h** is pronounced as in German *ich,* see above 1), **futatsu,** *two things,* as **ftats, chikai,** *near,* as **chkai.** The student should be quick to recognize these "fast" forms, but should only acquire the habit of using them after having mastered the material in the book.

THE ACCENT

12. The Japanese word-accent is one of pitch rather than of intensity (heaviness), as in English (compare the difference between English *insért* and *ínsert*). Since it therefore depends on pronouncing certain vowels in the word on a higher musical pitch (or musical note) than others, the student is advised to mimic the words spoken on the record as often and as accurately as he can. When in doubt about the pitch-configuration of a word, it is best to pronounce all of its vowels in monotone, that is, all syllables with even stress.

The pitch-accent can fall on any vowel in the word; in other words, the place of the pitch is unpredictable. The vowel of an accented syllable is uttered on a higher note

than the vowels of surrounding syllables, which are pronounced on a lower note.

For the purpose of accentuation, each sound which is
represented by a symbol of the Japanese syllabary (i.e.,
kana) must be treated as one syllable. Even if two vowels
are combined (see **10**), each vowel is treated as a separate
syllable (see Syllabary, p. 17, Row 1). The same applies
to word-final **n** (see Syllabary, Row 11) and medial **n**
before another consonant (see **4**; also Syllabary, p. 20,
No. 4).

In the examples below, a big dot signifies the word; and
a circle, its following particle. The syllable with a higher
note lies on the line, and the syllable with a lower note under
it. When the last syllable has a higher note than the particle
following it, it is indicated with an accent-sign (ˋ) as in **ha-shì
ga**, *the bridge* (the particle **ga** expresses the subject); in all
other cases a syllable with a higher note has an accent-sign
(ˊ), **há-shi ga**, *the chopsticks;* **sa-ká-ná ga**, *the fish*, etc.

(1)　Even the one-syllable word can have a pitch which
is easily discernible, if such a word is uttered with a particle following it:

		Examples:			
Type I	**hi ga**	**hi**	day	**e**	handle
		shi	poem	**cha**	tea, tea-plant
Type II	**hì ga**	**hì**	fire	**è**	picture
		shì	death	**tà**	rice field

In Type I the particle is pronounced on a higher note,
in Type II on a lower note.

(2)　In words with two syllables, we also recognize different types as shown below:

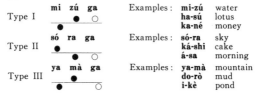

Type I	**mi zú ga**	Examples:	**mi-zú**	water
			ha-sú	lotus
			ka-né	money
Type II	**só ra ga**	Examples:	**só-ra**	sky
			ká-shi	cake
			á-sa	morning
Type III	**ya mà ga**	Examples:	**ya-mà**	mountain
			do-rò	mud
			i-kè	pond

The difference in pitch between Type I and Type II is very delicate, since the particle is pronounced with the same pitch as the last syllable of the word. In words of Type I and Type III, the last syllable is pronounced on a higher note; the difference is that in Type III the particle is on a lower note.

(3) Similarly four types are distinguishable in words with three syllables as follows:

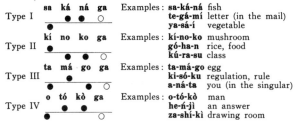

In this way, words with more than three syllables, e.g., **wa-tá-kú-shí,** *I, me* (Type I), **shí-n-se-tsu,** *kindness* (Type II), **ne-tó-ma-ri,** *stay overnight* (Type III), etc., also enter into consideration.

13. If the student finds it difficult not to accent one of the vowels of a word, he may pronounce the long vowels (**ā, ii, ū, ē, ō**) on a slightly higher pitch.

14. When listening to the recordings, the attentive student will observe that spoken Japanese makes a "choppy" or "staccato" impression. He will do well to imitate this feature by constantly keeping in mind the following four rules:

(1) Avoid the long "gliding" quality of the English long vowels (see **8 & 9**).

(2) Avoid the English unstressed vowel written **a** in **sofa** and **around** ; the Japanese word **atama,** *head*, contains three distinct **a**-vowels, all alike in quality.

(3) Remember that double consonants are pronounced twice as long as single consonants (see **2**).

(4) Avoid using heavy English stress when speaking Japanese. Follow the pattern of the native speaker.

15. The student with a keen ear will note that **p, t** and **k** are aspirated, i.e., followed by an *h*-sound; as in English. In addition, if a consonant is followed by **i**, it should be slightly palatalized; i.e., followed by a sound similar to the *y* in English *yeast* (see **5**).

THE SYLLABARY

16. The writing system and the syllabary (*kana*).

Japanese was originally written wholly in Chinese characters, which were borrowed during the fifth century A.D. By the ninth century, however, a system of syllabic notation developed, by which some forty-eight signs were made to transliterate sounds in the Japanese spoken tongue. The resultant syllabary is called **kana.** It takes two forms: **hiragana** and **katakana.**

Both Chinese and **kana** characters are used today in the Japanese system of writing. The former represent nouns, or the uninflected roots of verbs and adjectives; the latter inflected endings of verbs and adjectives. In addition, **kana** is used to write out such things as terms of politeness, constructional particles and certain adverbs which are not easily represented by Chinese characters. **Hiragana** is the more commonly used syllabary. **Katakana** is reserved primarily for use in official documents, children's books, telegrams, and in transliterating foreign names and words.

(1) The following is the Japanese syllabary systematically arranged which will be helpful for rapid comprehension of its sound-system:

HIRAGANA

	I	II	III	IV	V
1	a あ	i い	u う	e え	o お
2	ka か	ki き	ku く	ke け	ko こ
3	sa さ	shi (si) し	su す	se せ	so そ
4	ta た	chi (ti) ち	tsu (tu) つ	te て	to と
5	na な	ni に	nu ぬ	ne ね	no の
6	ha は	hi ひ	fu (hu) ふ	he へ	ho ほ
7	ma ま	mi み	mu む	me め	mo も
8	ya や	i い	yu ゆ	e え	yo よ
9	ra ら	ri り	ru る	re れ	ro ろ
10	wa わ	i [wi] ゐ	u う	e [we] ゑ	o [wo] を
11	n ん				

( ) See **17**, Rōmaji
〔 〕 See NOTE 2, p. 18

NOTE 1 : The rows are indicated by Arabic numerals and the classes by Roman numerals. There are eleven rows and five classes ; each row has five symbols, except the eleventh which has only one. Symbols 1/II, 1/IV and 1/III are the same as 8/II, 8/IV and 10/III respectively, making a total of forty-eight. In modern standard Japanese, 10/II, 10/IV and 10/V are identical in pronunciation to 1/II, 1/IV and 1/V respectively.

NOTE 2 : Formerly there were two additional syllables in the system, **kwa** and **gwa,** which have disappeared in standard Japanese.

The symbols 10/II, 10/IV and 10/V represent the old sounds **wi, we** and **wo** respectively. In this case the labialized consonant **w** is already obsolete.

(2)   There are also derivatives of rows 2, 3, 4 and 6.   They are slightly different in form, and represent the values shown below :

HARD and SOFT (6") Sounds of HIRAGANA

	I	II	III	IV	V
2'	ga が	gi ぎ	gu ぐ	ge げ	go ご
3'	za ざ	ji (zi) じ	zu ず	ze ぜ	zo ぞ
4'	da だ	ji (di) ぢ	zu (du) づ	de で	do ど
6'	ba ば	bi· び	bu ぶ	be べ	bo ぼ
6"	pa ば	pi び	pu ぶ	pe べ	po ぽ

NOTE : Although symbols 3'/II and 4'/II differ in form, they have the same value (**ji**) in modern standard Japanese. This is also the case with symbols 3'/III, and 4'/III (**zu**).

Japanese do not pronounce **zi, di** and **du** as **z** and **d** are pronounced in English *zeal, deal, do*, etc., because the consonant **z** is palatalized when followed by the vowel **i** ; and **d** is palatalized when followed by **i** or **u**. Due to this variation, row 3' has two different consonants, **z** and **j** ; and row 4' has three, **d, j** and **z**. (Compare rows 3 and 4, p. 17.)

(3) Several consonants are followed by the palatalized vowels **ya, yu** and **yo,** forming the compounds listed below:

KANA COMPOUNDS*

	I	III	V
2·	kya きゃ	kyu きゅ	kyo きょ
3·	sha (sya) しゃ	shu (syu) しゅ	sho (syo) しょ
4·	cha (tya) ちゃ	chu (tyu) ちゅ	cho (tyo) ちょ
5·	nya にゃ	nyu にゅ	nyo にょ
6·	hya ひゃ	hyu ひゅ	hyo ひょ
7·	mya みゃ	myu みゅ	myo みょ
9·	rya りゃ	ryu りゅ	ryo りょ
2··	gya ぎゃ	gyu ぎゅ	gyo ぎょ
3··	ja (zya/dya) じゃ	ju (zyu/dyu) じゅ	jo (zyo/dyo) じょ
4··	ja (zya/dya) ぢゃ	ju (zyu/dyu) ぢゅ	jo (zyo/dyo) ぢょ
6··	bya びゃ	byu びゅ	byo びょ
6···	pya ぴゃ	pyu ぴゅ	pyo ぴょ

* Each compound represents one syllable.

The symbols of rows 3·· and 4·· are different.   In

modern Japanese, however, 3"/I is identical with 4"/I, 3"/III with 4"/III and 3"/V with 4"/V in pronunciation.

(4) The double consonants, **pp, tt, kk** and **ss** (see **2**), e.g., **rippa**, *magnificent*, **shitta**, (I, you, he, etc.) *knew*, **kekka**, *result*, etc., are rendered by the symbol 4/III (**tsu**). It is written smaller when it appears within a word, as in the following examples:

kippu	きっぷ	ticket
yokatta	よかった	was good (see Grammar p. 97)
nikki	にっき	diary
massao	まっさお	completely blue, etc.

But the double nasal consonants, **mm** and **nn,** are designated by the symbol II/1 (**n**):

samman	さんまん (三万)	30,000 (see Grammar p. 98)
konna	こんな	such a (see Grammar p. 104)

17. Rōmaji.

Rōmaji is a general term covering systems of romanizing both Chinese and Japanese script. There are two systems of romanization in current use: the Hepburn and Nipponsiki Rōmaji. The latter system of spelling is given in the parentheses in the syllabary charts (see above **16**).

The Hepburn system was devised in 1885 and Nipponsiki Rōmaji some fifty years later. The government attempted without success to make Nipponsiki Rōmaji official. As a result, today few Japanese hold consistently to either one or the other systems of romanization; students of the language must therefore be prepared to meet both. Capitalization and division of words in Rōmaji vary widely.

THE INTONATION

(1) Generally speaking, affirmative and negative sentences do not have a rise or fall in pitch at the end.

For example:

Affirmative :	a- no hi-to wa ko-ko ni i- ma-su – – – – – – – – – –	He is here.
Negative :	a- no hi-to wa ko-ko ni i- ma-se -n – – – – – – – – – – –	He is not here.

(2) a. Interrogative sentences have a rise in pitch at the end whether or not the interrogative particle **ka** is used.

For example :

Interrogative with the particle **ka** :	**a- no hi-to wa ko-ko ni i- ma-su ka?** – – – – – – – – – – ‾ – –	Is he here ?
Interrogative without the particle **ka** :	**a- no hi-to wa ko-ko ni i- ma-su ?** – – – – – – – – – – ‾ –	Is he here ?

b. The same applies to negative-interrogative sentences.

For example :

Negative–Interrogative with the particle **ka** :	**a- no hi-to wa ko-ko ni i- ma-se -n ka?** – – – – – – – – – – ‾ – –	Is he not here ?
Negative–Interrogative without the particle **ka** :	**a- no hi-to wa ko-ko ni i- ma-se -n ?** – – – – – – – – – – ‾ –	Is he not here?

In an interrogative sentence with the particle **ka**, the last three syllables are, in most cases, pronounced with a rise in pitch.

(3) As a rule, the pitch of any given word is not altered by its combination with other words in sentences or phrases.

For example :

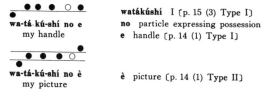

wa-tá·kú-shí no e my handle	**watákúshí** I [p. 15 (3) Type I] **no** particle expressing possession **e** handle [p. 14 (1) Type I]
wa-tá·kú-shí no è my picture	**è** picture [p. 14 (1) Type II]

In this example the word **e** *picture* has a higher note than the preceding four syllables, thus there are three different pitches.

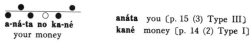

a-ná-ta no ka-né your money	**anáta** you [p. 15 (3) Type III] **kané** money [p. 14 (2) Type I]

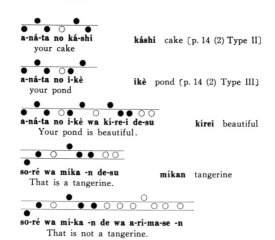

a-ná-ta no ká-shi · your cake — **káshi** cake [p. 14 (2) Type II]

a-ná-ta no i-kè · your pond — **ikè** pond [p. 14 (2) Type III]

a-ná-ta no i-kè wa kí-re-i de-su · Your pond is beautiful. — **kírei** beautiful

so-ré wa míka -n de-su · That is a tangerine. — **míkan** tangerine

so-ré wa mí-ka -n de wa a-rí-ma-se -n · That is not a tangerine.

THE LATIN ALPHABET IN JAPANESE

Often it is necessary to have words spelled out such as streets, cities, surnames, etc. Most Japanese who know English can generally be understood by an English speaker when pronouncing the letters of the Latin alphabet. However, Japanese who do not speak English generally pronounce the Latin alphabet as follows:

A	ei	J	jei	R	āru
B	bii	K	kei	S	esu
C	shii	L	eru	T	tei
D	dei	M	emu	U	yuu
E	ii	N	enu	V	bui
F	efu	O	oo	W	dabburu yuu
G	jii	P	pii	X	ekisu
H	eichi	Q	kyuu	Y	uai
I	ai			Z	zetto

Note especially : C, D, L, T, V, Z. Some individuals may have intermediate pronunciations between this system and standard English depending on their level of education.

BASIC SENTENCE PATTERNS

In each language there are a few types of sentences which are used more often than others in everyday speech.

On the basis of such sentences, one can form many others simply by replacing one or two of the words. The sentences selected to illustrate the basic patterns are short, useful and easy to memorize. Learning them before you enter the main section of Everyday Conversations will give you an idea of the structure of the language. Through them, you will also learn indirectly some of the most important grammatical categories and their function in the construction of sentences. This is, in fact, the natural way of learning a language—the way a child absorbs its native language by hearing, repeating and using the words and constructions.

Cross references have been supplied to establish a correlation between the Basic Sentence Patterns and the Outline of Grammar. The grammatical knowledge you will acquire from the basic sentences can thus be related to the systematic presentation of grammar.

There is no article in Japanese.

Strictly speaking no distinction is made between singular and plural forms, but there are certain suffixes which are used to indicate plurality (See Grammar 1-3).

AFFIRMATIVE STATEMENTS
(See Grammar ¶ 7, 9, 11, 12, 14, 32, 35-38, 44, 49)

私　　　　は　日本人　です。
Watakushi wa nihonjin desu.
I am a Japanese.

それ は 本 です。
Sore wa hon desu.
That is a book.

手紙　　が　きた。（きました。）
Tegami ga kita.（kimashita）
The letter has come. (polite)

電報　をうちましょう。
Dempō o uchimashō.
Let's send a telegram.

私　　　は　手紙　　を書きました。
Watakushi wa tegami o kakimashita.
I wrote a letter.

23

寒い　です。　　　　　　　雨　が　降っている。
Samui desu.　　　　　　**Ame ga futte iru.**
It is cold.　　　　　　　　*It is raining.*

私　　は　あす京都　へ行きます。
Watakushi wa asu Kyōto e ikimasu.
I am going to Kyoto tomorrow.

兄　は　アメリカ　から　小包　　を送って　くれました。
Ani wa Amerika kara kozutsumi o okutte kuremashita.
My elder brother has sent me a package from America.

NEGATIVES
(See Grammar ¶ 33, 36, 42, 47)

私　　　　　は　日本人　では　ない。　じゃない。
Watakushi wa nihonjin dewa nai.　　**ja nai**
I am not a Japanese. (less polite)　　(informal)

では　ありません。
de wa arimasen.
(polite)

手紙　　が　きません　でした。　　こなかった。
Tegami ga kimasen deshita.　　**konakatta.**
The letter has not come. (polite)　(less polite)

雨が　降っていません。　　　　　いない。
Ame ga futte imasen.　　　　　**inai.**
It is not raining.　　　　　　　(less polite)

きのう行きませんでした。　　　（行かなかった。
Kinō ikimasen deshita.　　　　**ikanakatta.**
I didn't go yesterday.　　　　　(less polite)

歌舞伎　を見た　こと　は　ない。
Kabuki o mita koto wa nai.
*I have never seen a **Kabuki** play.*

こんな　本　は　読みません。　　（読まない。
Konna hon wa yomimasen.　　　**yomanai**
I don't read this kind of a book.　(less polite)

私　　　は　日本語　が　わかります。
Watakushi wa nihongo ga wakarimasu.
I understand Japanese.

彼　は　日本語　が　話せません。　　　（話せない。）
Kare wa nihongo ga hanasemasen.　　**hanasenai**
He can't speak Japanese.　　　　　　　(less polite)

SIMPLE QUESTIONS AND ANSWERS
(See Grammar ¶ 10, 12, 32, 49-51,)

誰　です　か。
Dare desu ka?
Who is it (he, she)? or *Who are you (they)?*

友達　　です。
Tomodachi desu.
It is my (his, her, your or their) friend.

お父さんです。
Otōsan desu.
It is my (his, her, your or their) father.

Since the subject of the sentence is implicitly expressed by the context in Japanese, it is often unnecessary and likely to be omitted.

The predicate verb **desu** does not distinguish the subject; it retains the same form for all persons.

何　です　か。
Nan desu ka?
What is it (this or that)? or *What are these? etc.*

家　です。
Ie desu.
It is a house. These (or those) are houses.

Nan is the elliptical form of **nani** (*what*).

どこ　です　か。
Doko desu ka?
Where is it?

東京　です。
Tōkyō desu.
It is in Tokyo.

The English preposition *in* is not expressed in such a case in Japanese.

いつ 日本　へ着きます　か。
Itsu Nihon e tsukimasu ka?
When do I (we, you or they) arrive in Japan? or *When does he (she or it) arrive in Japan?*

あす 着きます。
Asu tsukimasu.
I (we, you or they) arrive tomorrow or *he (she or it) arrives tomorrow.*

In Japanese the predicate verb is placed at the end of a sentence, unless the interrogative particle **ka** or other type of particle is present.

あれは 誰　です か。
Are wa dare desu ka?
Who is that?

あれは　お母さんです。
Are wa okāsan desu.
That is my (his, her, our, your or their) moth

これ は 誰　です か。
Kore wa dare desu ka?
Who is this? or *Who are these?*

これ は 生徒 です。
Kore wa seito desu.
This is a pupil. or *These are pupils.*

それ は 何　です か。
Sore wa nan desu ka?
What is that?

それ は 庭 です。
Sore wa niwa desu.
That is a garden.

あれは 何 です か。
Are wa nan desu ka?
What is that? or *What are those?*

あれは 自動車 です。
Are wa jidōsha desu.
That is an automobile. or *Those are automobiles.*

ここ は どこ です か。
Koko wa doko desu ka?
What is here (this place)?

ここ は 学校 です。
Koko wa gakkō desu.
This place is a (or the) school.

そこ は どこ です か。
Soko wa doko desu ka?
What is there (that place)?

そこ は 駅 です。
Soko wa eki desu.
That place is a station.

あそこ は どこ です か。
Asoko wa doko desu ka?
What is the place over there?

あそこ は 公園 です。
Asoko wa kōen desu.
The place over there is a park.

あそこ に いる 人達 は 誰 です か。
Asoko ni iru hitotachi wa dare desu ka?
Who are those people over there?

学生 達 です。
Gakusei-tachi desu.
They are students.

PRONOUNS AND USE OF PARTICLES
(Grammar ¶ 2-4, 7-10, 13, 15-17, 34-38, 49, 52, 53, 56, 57)

あなた は 誰 です か。
Anata wa dare desu ka?
Who are you?

私　　　は 旅行者 です。
Watakushi wa ryokōsha desu.
I am a tourist.

あなた がた は アメリカ 人 です か。
Anata gata wa Amerika-jin desu ka?
Are you Americans?

いいえ, 私　　達　は イギリス人 です。
Iie, watakushi tachi wa Igirisu-jin desu.
No, we are Englishmen (or *Englishwomen*).

彼　は 誰 です か。
Kare wa dare desu ka?
Who is he?

あの かた は どなた です か。
Ano kata wa donata desu ka?
Who is he (or *she*)? (*lit., Who is that person?*)

彼　は 友達　　です。
Kare wa tomodachi desu.
He is (*my*) *friend.*

あの かた は 先生　です。
Ano kata wa sensei desu.
He (or *she*) *is* (*our*) *teacher.*

この　かた も 先生　です か。
Kono kata mo sensei desu ka?
Is this person also a teacher?

はい, そうです。　　ええそうです。
Hai, sō desu or **Ē, sō desu.**
Yes, he (or *she*) *is.*

Ē is more commonly used than **hai** for *yes*. Although **hai** occurs in ordinary conversation, it is generally reserved for rigid formal conversations, e.g., between teacher and student, master and servant, officer and soldier, etc.

The Japanese word **kata**, *person*, expresses the singular and **gata**, *persons*, the plural. Both forms follow another word and only apply to the second and third persons.

これ は お父さんの 靴 です か。
Kore wa otōsan no kutsu desu ka?
Are these your father's shoes?

ええそうです。
Ē, sō desu.
Yes, they are.

あれ は あなたの お弟さん の 奥さん です か。
Are wa anata no otōto-san no okusan desu ka?
Is she (lit., that) your younger brother's wife?

ええそうです。
Ē, sō desu.
Yes, she is.

それ は お母さんの 傘 です か。
Sore wa okāsan no kasa desu ka?
Is that your mother's umbrella (or parasol)?

はい そうです。
Hai, sō desu.
Yes, it is.

どれ が あなたの 鉛筆 です か。
Dore ga anata no empitsu desu ka?
Which is your pencil? or *Which are your pencils?*

これ が 私 の 鉛筆 です。
Kore ga watakushi no empitsu desu.
This is my pencil. or *These are my pencils.*

あの かた の お姉さんは 京都　にいますか。
Ano kata no onē-san wa Kyōto ni imasu ka?
Is that person's elder sister in Kyoto?

ええ，京都 にいます。
Ē, Kyōto ni imasu.
Yes, she is in Kyoto.

その 男　の 子供　は 音楽　を 聞きます　か。
Sono otoko no kodomo wa ongaku o kikimasu ka?
Does that boy listen to music?

はい，聞きます。
Hai, kikimasu.
Yes, he does.

あなた は　どこ で ごはん を 食べます　か。
Anata wa doko de gohan o tabemasu ka?
Where do you take a meal?

ここ で 食べます。
Koko de tabemasu.
I take (it) here.

この 部屋 で 食べます。
Kono heya de tabemasu.
I take (it) in this room.

あの 人 は 本 をどこ で 読みます　か。
Ano hito wa hon o doko de yomimasu ka?
Where does that person read a book (or books)?

そこ で 読みます。
Soko de yomimasu.
He (or she) reads there.

この 子（供） は どこ まで 歩きました　か。
Kono ko (domo) wa doko made arukimashita ka?
How far (lit., to where) did this child walk?

公園 まで 歩きました。
Kōen made arukimashita.
He (or she) walked as far as the park.

あなた は いつ 本 を読みます か。
Anata wa itsu hon o yomimasu ka?
When do you read a book (or *books*)?

朝 **Asa** *in the morning*		*in the morning.*
昼 **Hiru** *in the daytime*	読みます。 **yomimasu**. *I read*	*I read*	*in the daytime.*
晩 **Ban** *in the evening*		*in the evening.*

いつ まで 日本 に いました か。
Itsu made Nihon ni imashita ka?
Until when were you in Japan?

五 月 の 初め まで いました。
Go-gatsu no hajime made imashita.
I was (there) *until the beginning of May.*

NEGATIVE QUESTIONS
(See Grammar ¶ 33, 36-38, 47)

これ は あなたの 帽子 では ありませんか。
Kore wa anata no bōshi de wa arimasen ka?
Is it not your hat (or *cap*)?

いいえ, 私 の (物) です。
Iie, watakushi no (mono) desu.
Yes, it is mine.

はい, そうでは ありません。
Hai, sō de wa arimasen.
No, it is not.

あなた は 新聞 を 読みません か。
Anata wa shimbun o yomimasen ka?
Don't you read a newspaper (or *newspapers*)?

いいえ, 読みます。
Iie, yomimasu.
Yes, I read.

ええ, 読みません。
Ē, yomimasen.
No, I do not read.

As a rule English *yes* and *no* correspond to Japanese **hai** (or **ē**) and **iie** respectively. Note that these correspondences are reversed in response to a negative question.

あの かた は みかん を食べません か。
Ano kata wa mikan o tabemasen ka?
Does not he (or *she*) *eat a tangerine?*

いいえ, 食べます。
Iie, tabemasu.
Yes, he (or *she*) *does.*

はい, 食べません。
Hai, tabemasen.
No, he (or *she*) *does not.*

この 靴 は 好きでは ありませんか。
Kono kutsu wa suki de wa arimasen ka?
Don't you like these shoes?

いいえ, 好き です。
Iie, suki desu.
Yes, I like them.

ええ, 好きでは ありません。
Ē, suki de wa arimasen.
No, I don't like them.

りんご は ありませんか。
Ringo wa arimasen ka?
Don't you have apples?

いいえ, あります。
Iie, arimasu.
Yes, we have.

はい, ありません。
Hai, arimasen.
No, we have not.

この　列車　は　五時には　名古屋　に　着きません　か。
Kono ressha wa go ji niwa Nagoya ni tsukimasen ka?
Does not this train arrive in Nagoya at five o'clock?

いいえ, 着きます。
Iie,　tsukimasu.
Yes, it does.

はい, 着きません。
Hai, tsukimasen.
No, it does not.

あなた の 妹　さんは まだ 来ません か。
Anata no imōto-san wa mada kimasen ka?
Has not your younger sister come yet?

いいえ, もう 来ました。
Iie,　mō kimashita.
Yes, she has come already.

ええ, まだ 来ません。
Ē,　mada kimasen.
No, she has not come yet.

誰　が まだ 来ません か。
Dare ga mada kimasen ka?
Who has not come yet?

あの 人　（かた）の おじさんが まだ 来ません。
Ano hito (*or* kata) no oji-san ga mada kimasen.
*His (*or* her) uncle has not yet come.*

ADJECTIVES
(See Grammar ¶ 22-26, 28)

若い　人　が います。
Wakai hito ga imasu.
*There is a young man (*or* woman). or There are young men
(*or* women).*

若い　人　は　いません。
Wakai hito wa imasen.
There is not a young man (or *woman*). or *There are not young men* (or *women*).

赤い　花　が　あります。
Akai hana ga arimasu.
There is a red flower. or *There are red flowers.*

きれいな　家が　ありません。
Kirei na ie ga arimasen.
There is not a beautiful house. or *There are not beautiful houses.*

この　本　は　新しい　です。
Kono hon wa atarashii desu.
This book is new. or *These books are new.*

あの　本　は　おもしろかった。
Ano hon wa omoshirokatta.
That book was interesting. or *Those books were interesting.*

あの　本　は　おもしろく　なかった。
Ano hon wa omoshiroku nakatta.
That book was not interesting. or *Those books were not interesting.*

この　魚　は　まずい。
Kono sakana wa mazui.
This fish is tasteless. or *These fishes are tasteless.*

それ　は　新しい　です　か。
Sore wa atarashii desu ka?
Is that new?

いいえ，古い　です。
Iie, furui desu.
No, it is old.

まあ，きれいな　庭　だこ
Mā, kirei na niwa da kote!
Oh, what a beautiful garden!

映画 は とても 良かった。
Eiga wa totemo yokatta.
The movie was very good.

その かた は もう 若く は ありませんか。
Sono kata wa mō wakaku wa arimasen ka?
Isn't that person still young?

いいえ, まだ 若い です。
Iie, mada wakai desu.
Yes, he (or she) is still young.

その 自動車 は 新しい では ありませんか。
Sono jidōsha wa atarashii de wa arimasen ka?
Isn't that automobile new?

いいえ, 新しい です。
Iie, atarashii, desu.
Yes, it is new.

ええ, 新しく は ありません。
Ē, atarashiku wa arimasen.
No, it is not new.

COMPARISON
(See Grammar ¶ 26 & 27)

田中 さんは クラス で 一番 美しい かた です。
Tanaka-san wa kurasu de ichiban utsukushii kata desu.
Miss Tanaka is the most beautiful girl (lit., person) in the class.

思った より この 本 は 高かった。
Omotta yori kono hon wa takakatta.
This book was more expensive than I had expected.

あの かた は とても 親切 です。
Ano kata wa totemo shinsetsu desu.
That person (or he, she) is very kind.

富士山 は 日本 で最も 有名 な 山 です。
Fujisan wa Nippon de mottomo yūmei na yama desu.
Mt. Fuji is the most famous mountain in Japan.

あなた は 私 より頭 が 良い。
Anata wa watakushi yori atama ga ii.
You are smarter (lit., head is good) than I.

彼 は なか なか 有望 な 青年 です。
Kare wa naka-naka yūbō na seinen desu.
He is a very promising youth.

この 店 の ほうが 安い。
Kono mise no hō ga yasui.
This store is cheaper. (lit., This store's direction is cheap.)

Hō, literally, *general direction* or *side*, is also used to express comparison.

IMPERATIVES
(Polite form of imperatives, See Grammar ¶ 45)

新聞 を買ってきて 下さい。
Shimbun o katte kite kudasai.
Please buy (or *bring*) *me a newspaper* (or *newspapers*).

新聞 を買ってくれ。
Shimbun o katte kure. (*informal*)
Buy me a newspaper (or *newspapers*).

The informal particle **kure** is never used by women.

本 を読んで 下さい。
Hon o yonde kudasai.
Please read a book to me.

電話 を掛けて 下さい。
Denwa o kakete kudasai.
Please give me a ring.

そんな 大きな 音 を立てないで 下さい。
Sonna ōkina oto o tatenai de kudasai.
Please don't make so much noise.

それ を拾って くれ。
Sore o hirotte kure,
Pick that up for me.

NUMBERS
(See Grammar ¶ 29-31)

今　何時 です か。
Ima nanji desu ka?
What time is it now?

二時半 です。
Niji han desu.
Half past two.

そこ には いくつ りんごが ありますか。
Soko niwa ikutsu ringo ga arimasu ka?
How many apples are there?

一つ　　二つ　　三つ　　四つ　　五つ　　五つ。　 あります。
Hitotsu, futatsu, mittsu, yottsu, itsutsu. Itsutsu arimasu.
One, two, three, four, five. There are five (apples).

いつ着きます　か。
Itsu tsukimasu ka?
When are you arriving?

十月　　三十日　に着きます。
Jū-gatsu san-jū nichi ni tsukimasu.
I shall arrive on October 30th.

この　着物　は いくらです か。
Kono kimono wa ikura desu ka?
How much is this kimono?

三千五百　円 です。
San-zen go-hyaku en desu.
It is 3,500 yen.

EXCLAMATIONS AND INTERJECTIONS

あああ
Ā (*mild surprise*)
Oh!

ああつかれた。
Ā tsukareta!
Oh, I'm tired!

ああうれしい。
Ā ureshii!
How glad I am!

あんなこと。
Anna koto
Such a thing!

あんなこと 言って。
Anna koto itte!
Saying such a thing!

あんなこと して。
Anna koto shite!
Doing such a thing!

あら
Ara
(*surprise; generally used by women*)

あら 美しい こと。
Ara utsukushii koto!
Oh, how beautiful!

あら まあ
Ara mā!
Oh, my!

ちょっと
Chotto
Say!

ちょっと 駅 は どこ です か。
Chotto, eki wa doko desu ka?
Say, where is the station?

で は じゃあ
De wa *or* **jā**
Well (let's...) or *well then*

で は （じゃあ）行きましよう。
De wa (*or* **jā**), **ikimashō.**
Well, let's go.

じゃあ（で は） 失礼します。
Jā (or **de wa**), **shitsureishimasu.**
Well then, I shall excuse myself. or *I'll say good-bye.*

どうも
Dōmo
(*polite hesitation; being at a loss as to how to begin thanking, requesting* or *saying something.*)

どうも 有難とう。
Dōmo arigatō.
I thank you very much.

どうも 困りました。
Dōmo komarimashita.
I am in a fix.

まあ
Mā
(*sometimes expresses surprise*) *oh!* or (*hesitation*) *let me see, well, now* or (*emphatic*) *do.*

まあ驚いた。
Mā odoroita!
Oh, what a surprise!

まあ行かずに おきましょう。
Mā yukazuni okimashō.
Well, I would rather not go.

まあ考えて おきましょう。
Mā kangaete okimashō.
Well now, I'll think about it.

まあお入り 下さい。
Mā o-hairi kudasai.
Do come in.

もし もし
Moshi-moshi
Hello (*on the telephone*), *say* or *excuse me* (*to call attention*).

On the telephone:

もし もし どなた です か。
Moshi-moshi donata desu ka?
Hello, who is this? or *Who is speaking?*

もし　もし　こちら　は　鈴木　です。
Moshi-moshi kochira wa Suzuki desu.
Miss (Mr. or Mrs.) Suzuki speaking. or This is Suzuki.

もし　もし，博物館　　　は　どこ　です　か。
Moshi-moshi, hakubutsukan wa doko desu ka?
Excuse me, but where is the museum?

なるほど
Naruhodo
Indeed!, Is that so!, or Well! (used by men only)

なるほど　君　の　言うこと　は　正しい　です。
Naruhodo, kimi no yū koto wa tadashii desu.
Indeed, you are right.

そうです　ねえ。
Sō desu nē.
Let me see.

さあねえ，どうしましょう。
Sā nē, dō shimashō.
Let me see, what shall I do? or What shall we do?

さて　　　　　　　　さて，出かける　こと　に　しょうか。
Sate　　　　　　　**Sate, dekakeru koto ni shiyō ka?**
well　　　　　　　　*Well, shall we start going?*

そして　　　　　　　そして　次　は。
Soshite　　　　　　**Soshite tsugi wa?**
and then　　　　　　*And then what's next?*

それ　では　　それ　じゃ
Sore de wa *or* **sore jā**
in that case, let's.....

それ　じゃ　（では）映画　へ行きましょう。
Sore jā (*or* **de wa**) **eiga e ikimashō.**
In that case, let's go to the movies.

EVERYDAY CONVERSATIONS
BASIC EXPRESSIONS

お早う ございます
Ohayō gozaimasu.
Good morning.

今日 は
Kon-nichi wa
Good afternoon.

今晩 は
Kom-ban wa
Good evening.

さよなら
Sayonara
Good-bye.

(どうも)ありがとうございます
(Dōmo) arigatō gozaimasu.
Thank you (very much).

どう致しまして
Dō itashimashite.
You are welcome.
Don't mention it.

どうぞ
Dōzo
Please (entreating).

どれ   どちら
Dore? *or* **Dochira?**
Which?

お願い します
Onegai shimasu.
Please.

失礼   します
Shitsurei shimasu.
Excuse me. or *Pardon me.*
(lit., I am commiting a breach
of etiquette.)

御免   下さい
Gomen kudasai.
Excuse me. or *Pardon me.*
(lit., Your forgiveness please.)

恐れ   入ります
Osore irimasu.
Excuse me. or *Thank you.*
(lit., I am awestruck.)

いくら です か
Ikura desu ka?
How much is it?

どこ (へ)   ここ   そこ
Doko (e)?[1] **Koko.** **Soko.**
(To) where? Here.   There.

なぜ
Naze?
Why?

[1]See Grammar, Particles : p. 93 (para. 12).

いつ？
Itsu?
When?

何時（に）？[1]
Nan-ji (ni)?[1]
(At) what time?

何
Nani?
What?

私　　　は　山本　　と　申します。
Watakushi wa Yamamoto to mōshimasu.[2]
My name is (Mrs.) Yamamoto.

私　　　は　石田　　です。
Watakushi wa Ishida desu.[2]
I am (Mr.) Ishida.

英語　が　出来ます　　か。
Eigo ga dekimasu ka?
Do you speak English?

はい, 少し　　　出来ます。
Hai, sukoshi dekimasu.
Yes, I speak it a little.

日本語　　が　出来ます　　か。
Nihongo ga dekimasu ka?
Do you speak Japanese?

いいえ, 日本語　　が　出来ません。
Iie,　Nihongo ga dekimasen.
No, I don't speak Japanese.

もう一度　言つて下さい。
Mō ichido itte　kudasai.
I beg your pardon. (lit., Will you say [it] again?)

もっと　ゆっくり　話して　　下さい。
Motto yukkuri hanashite kudasai.
Please speak more slowly.

分りません。
Wakarimasen.
I don't understand.

---

[1]See Grammar, Particles: p. 94 for the use of postpositions.
[2]See Grammar, Personal Pronouns: p. 105 for the omission of subject.

ご機嫌　いかが です か。
Gokigen ikaga desu ka?
How are you?

GETTING TO KNOW YOU

中村　　　と 申します。
Nakamura to mōshimasu.
My name is (Mr.) Nakamura.

こちら　は　家内 です。
Kochira wa kanai desu.
This is my wife.

岡田　さん を 御紹介　　します。
Okada San o go-shōkai[1] shimasu.
This is Miss Okada.　(introduction)　(lit., I will introduce
Miss Okada.)

初めまして。　　どうぞ 宜しく。
Hajimemashite.　Dōzo yoroshiku.
I am pleased to meet you.

日本　へ は　初めて　です か。
Nippon e wa hajimete desu ka?
Is it your first trip to Japan?

いいえ二度目 です。
Iie,　nido-me desu.
No, the second trip.

去年　　も　参りました。
Kyonen mo mairimashita.
I was also here last year.

御旅行　は　どうですか。
Go-ryokō wa dō desu ka?[1]
How are you enjoying your trip?

日本　が 大 好き です 京都　は　特　に すばらしい です。
Nippon ga dai-suki desu, Kyōto wa toku ni subarashii desu.
I like Japan very much; Kyoto is especially beautiful.
(lit., Kyoto is especially splendid or excellent.)

見物　　に いらっ'ゃったの です か。
Kembutsu ni irasshatta　no desu ka?
Are you here for sightseeing?

---

[1]See Grammar, Formal Language: pp. 107-108 for the use of honorifics.

はい, そうです。
Hai, sō desu.
Yes, I am.

こちら　に いつ 迄　ご 滞在　です か。
Kochira ni itsu made go-taizai[1] desu ka?
How long will you stay in this country?

三　カ月　程　居ります。
Sanka getsu hodo orimasu.
I will stay here about three months.

お宅　は どちら です か。
O-taku[1] wa dochira desu ka?
Where is your home?

宅　は ニューヨーク市　です。東京　と よく 似てます。
Taku wa New York Shi desu. Tōkyō to yoku nitemasu.
My home is in New York City.   It is very similar to Tokyo.

当方　へお出での 節　は どうぞ お立ち寄り 下さい。
Tōhō e oide no setsu wa, dōzo o-tachiyori[1] kudasai.
When you come my way, please get in touch with me.

COUNTING[2]

一	四	七	十
ichi	**shi**	**shichi**	**jū**
one	*four*	*seven*	*ten*
二	五	八	十一
ni	**go**	**hachi**	**jū-ichi**
two	*five*	*eight*	*eleven*
三	六	九	
san	**roku**	**ku** *or* **kyū**	
three	*six*	*nine*	

---

[1] See Grammar, Formal Language: pp. 107-108 for the use of honorifics.
[2] See Grammar, Cardinal Numbers: pp. 98-99 for detailed reference.

二十二
nijū-ni
twenty-two

六十六
rokujū-roku
sixty-six

百
hyaku
a hundred

三十三
sanjū-san
thirty-three

七十七
shichijū-shichi
seventy-seven

千
sen
a thousand

四十四
yonjū-shi
forty-four

八十八
hachijū-hachi
eighty-eight

一万
ichiman
ten thousand

五十五
gojū-go
fifty-five

九十九
kujū-ku *or* **kyūju-kyū**
ninety-nine

THE CLOCK AND THE CALENDAR

何時　です　か。
Nan-ji desu ka?
What time is it?

一時　です。
Ichiji desu.
It is one o'clock.

四時半　です。
Yoji-han desu.
It is half past four.

五時　十分　前　です。
Goji juppun mae desu.
It is ten minutes to five.

七時　二十分　（過ぎ）です。
Shichiji nijuppun (sugi) desu.
It is twenty minutes (past) seven.

今日　は　何　曜日　です　か。
Kyō wa nan yōbi desu ka?
What day of the week is it today?

日　曜日,　月　曜日,　火 曜日,　水 曜日,　木　曜日,
Nichi-yōbi,　Getsu-yōbi,　Ka-yōbi, Sui-yōbi,　Moku-yōbi,
It is Sunday, Monday,　　Tuesday, Wednesday, Thursday,
金　曜日,　土 曜日　です。
Kin-yōbi, Do-yōbi　desu.
Friday,　　Saturday.

今日　は　何　日　です　か。
Kyō[1] wa nan-nichi desu ka?
What date is it today? (lit., What is today's date?)

一　月　一日,　　二 月　二日,　　三　月　三日,
Ichi-gatsu tsuitachi, Ni-gatsu futsuka, San-gatsu mikka,
It is January 1st,　　February 2nd,　　March 3rd,

四 月　四日,　　五 月　五日,　　六月六日,
Shi-gatsu yokka,　Go-gatsu itsuka,　Roku-gatsu muika,
April 4th,　　May 5th,　　June 6th,

七　月　七日,　　　　八　月　八日,
Shichi-gatsu nanoka,　　Hachi-gatsu yōka,
July 7th,　　　　August 8th,

九 月　九日,　　　　十 月　十日,
Ku-gatsu kokonoka,　　Jū-gatsu tōka,
September 9th,　　October 10th,

十一　月　十一　日,　　十二 月　十二 日　です。
Jūichi-gatsu jūichi-nichi, Jūni-gatsu jūni-nichi desu.
November 11th,　　December 12th.

四季　は　春,　夏,　秋　と　冬　です。
Shiki wa haru, natsu, aki to fuyu desu.
The four seasons are spring, summer, autumn and winter.

日本　の 春　と 秋　は　綺麗 です。
Nippon no haru to aki wa kirei desu.
The spring and autumn are beautiful in Japan.

---

[1]See Key to Pronunciation, The Syllabary (2/V): p. 19.

日本 の 祭日 は 新 年 の 日(一 月 一日),
Nippon no saijitsu wa Shin-nen no Hi (Ichi-gatsu tsuitachi),
Japanese national holidays are New Year's Day (Jan. 1st.),

成 人 の 日(一 月 十五日),
Sei-jin no Hi (Ichi-gatsu jūgo-nichi),
Youth's Day (January 15th),

春分 の 日(三 月 二十一 日),
Shumbun no Hi (San-gatsu nijūichi-nichi),
the Spring Equinox (March 21st),

天 皇 誕生 日(四 月 二十九 日),
Ten-nō Tanjō-bi (Shi-gatsu nijūku-nichi),
the Emperor's Birthday (April 29th),

憲法 発布 の 日 (五 月 三日),
Kempō Happu no Hi (Go-gatsu mikka),
Constitution Day (May 3rd),

子供 の 日(五 月 五月),
Kodomo no Hi (Go-gatsu itsuka),
Children's Day (May 5th),

文化 の 日(十一 月 三日) と 勤労 感謝 の 日
Bunka no Hi (Jūichi-gatsu mikka) to Kinrō Kansha no Hi
Culture Day (November 3rd), and Labor Thanksgiving

(十一 月 二十三 日) です。
(Jūichi-gatsu nijūsan-nichi) desu.
Day (November 23rd).

天気 は どうです か。
Tenki wa dō desu ka?
How is the weather?

よい 天気 です。
Yoi tenki desu.
It is fine.

曇って います。
Kumotte imasu.
It is cloudy.

雨 が 降っています。
Ame ga futte imasu.
It is raining.

STRANGER IN TOWN

ちょっと お伺い　　しますか　最寄り の　交通公社　へどう
Chotto o-ukagai[1] shimasu, moyori no Kōtsūkōsha e dō
行きます か。
ikimasu ka?
May I ask you how to get to the nearest Japan Travel Bureau?

四つ谷　　駅　で中央　線 に 乗って六つ　　目 で降りなさい。
Yotsuya Eki de Chūō-sen ni notte muttsu-me de orinasai.
東京　　駅　の すぐ 前　にあります。　　駅　には 全部
Tōkyō Eki no sugu mae ni arimasu.　Eki niwa zembu
日本語　　と ローマ字で（方向　が）書いてあります から すぐ
Nihongo to Rōmaji de (hōkō ga) kaite arimasu kara sugu
わかります。
wakarimasu.
Take the Chuo Line at Yotsuya Station and get off at the sixth stop. There is one just in front of Tokyo Station. You will easily find (the directions) at train stations because they are written both in Japanese script and in Romanization.

もっと ゆっくり 話して　下さい。
Motto yukkuri hanashite kudasai.
Please speak more slowly.

もう一度　言って 下さい。
Mō ichido itte　kudasai.
I beg your pardon. (lit., Will you say [it] again?)

傘　を電車　に 忘れました。　　どうしましょうか。
Kasa o densha ni wasuremashita. Dō shimashō ka?
I left my umbrella in the train.　What shall I do?

駅　の 遺失物　　係　　へ 届けなさい。
Eki no ishitsubutsu-gakari[2] e todokenasai.
(Why don't you) report it to the lost-and-found office in the station?

---

[1]See Grammar, Formal Language: pp. 107-108 for the use of honorifics.
[2]See Key to Pronunciation, Alternations of Consonants: pp. 10-11.

移民 局 へ行きたい の です。
Imin-kyoku e ikitai no desu.
I would like to go to the Immigration Office.

書いて あげます から これ をタクシー の 運転手 に 見せ
Kaite agemasu kara kore o takushi no untenshu ni mise
なさい。
nasai.
I will write it for you so that you can show it to a taxi-driver.

アメリカ 大使館 へどう 行きます か。
Amerika Taishikan e dō ikimasu ka?
How can I get to the American Embassy?

三十五 番 の 都電 に 乗って終点 で 降りなさい。それ
Sanjūgo-ban no toden ni notte shūten de orinasai. Sore
から 二丁 程 北 へ歩いて 虎の門 に 出ると
kara ni-chō hodo kita e aruite Toranomon ni deruto
アメリカ 大使館 は すぐ 左 側 です。
Amerika Taishikan wa sugu hidari-gawa desu.
Take a No. 35 streetcar here and get off at the last stop. Then walk about two blocks north to Toranomon. The American Embassy is on the left.

買物 をしたいの です が どこ か 教えて 下さい。
Kaimono o shitai no desu ga, doko ka oshiete kudasai.
I would like to do some shopping here; could you tell me where I should go?

デパートが よろしい でしよう。何でも あります。
Depāto ga yoroshii deshō. Nandemo arimasu.
Department stores are suitable. You can get anything there.

ABOARD SHIP

キャビンクラス です。
Kyabin kurasu desu.
I am in cabin class.

船室　　は　六十　一　号　です。
Senshitsu wa rokujū-ichi gō desu.
Your stateroom is No. 61.

案　内　して　下さい。
Annai shite kudasai.
Direct me, please.

荷物　　　を船室　　へ運んで——下さい。
Nimotsu o senshitsu e hakonde kudasai.
Take the baggage to my stateroom, please.

食事　　は　何時　です　か。
Shokuji wa nanji desu ka?
At what time are meals served?

朝　は　八時　半，昼　は　一時，夕食　　は　六時　です。
Asa wa hachiji han, hiru wa ichiji, yūshoku wa rokuji desu.
それから　お茶　が　十時と　三時　に　あります。全部　　鐘　で
Sorekara o-cha[1] ga jūji to sanji ni arimasu. Zembu kane de
お知らせ　します。
o-shirase[1] shimasu.
*Breakfast is at half past eight, lunch is at one o'clock, and
dinner is at six o'clock. And there are teas at ten o'clock and
three o'clock. All will be announced by gong.*

毎晩　　五時に　お風呂　へ入りたいの　です。
Maiban goji ni o-furo e hairitai no desu.
I would like to take a bath every evening at five o'clock.

具合　が　悪い　です。船酔い　らしい　です。
Guai ga warui desu. Funayoi rashii desu.
I don't feel well. I might be seasick.

医務室　　へ行ってごらんなさい。デッキ C に　あります。
Imu-shitsu e itte goran-nasai. Dekki C ni arimasu.
I would suggest you go to the clinic. It is on Deck C.

いつ　横浜　　へ　着きます　か。
Itsu Yokohama e tsukimasu ka?
When do we arrive at Yokohama?

---

[1]See Grammar, Formal Language: pp. 107-108 for the use of honorifics.

八月　　　　十八　　　日　の　午前　六時　に　入港　の
Hachi-gatsu jū-hachi nichi no gozen rokuji ni nyūkō no
予定　です。
yotei desu.
We are expected to dock there at six o'clock in the morning on August 18th.

PLANE TRAVEL

ホンコン　　へ　行きたいのです。
Hongkong e ikitai no desu.
I would like to go to Hong Kong.

日本　　　航空　の　定期　航路　が　あります。
Nippon Kōkū no teiki kōro ga arimasu.
Japan Air Lines has regular flights there.

何時間　　　かかります　　か。
Nan-jikan kakarimasu ka?
How long does it take?

七時間　　　です。
Shichijikan desu.
It takes seven hours.

では　来週　金曜日　の　飛行機　に　予約　して　下さい。
Dewa, raishū Kin-yōbi no hikōki ni yoyaku shite kudasai.
Well, please reserve a seat on the next Friday flight.

荷物　　　は　どうです　か。
Nimotsu wa dō desu ka?
How about the baggage?

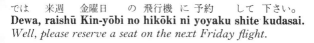

四十四　　　ポンド　迄　　ただ　です。
Yonjū-yon pondo made tada desu.
You are allowed forty-four pounds.

いつ　飛行場　へ来ましようか。
Itsu hikōjō e kimashō ka?
When do I have to come to the airport?

（飛行機 の）出発　　一時間　前　に 来て 下さい。
(Hikōki no) shuppatsu ichijikan mae ni kite kudasai.
Please be there one hour before the (plane's) departure.

東京　の 飛行場 は 何　と 言いますか。
Tōkyō no hikōjō wa nan to iimasu ka?
What is the name of the airport of Tokyo?

羽田　　国際　　　空港　と 言います。世界 の 二十 くらいの
Haneda Kokusai Kūkō to iimasu. Sekai no nijū kurai n
航空会社　　が 乗り入れて います。
kōkū-gaisha[1] ga noriirete imasu.
It is called Haneda International Airport. Nearly twent
airlines of the world have flights there.

GOING THROUGH CUSTOMS

荷物　　を 開けて 下さい。
Nimotsu o akete kudasai.
Open your baggage, please.

必需品　　　以外 お持ち　です　か。
Hitsujuhin igai o-mochi[2] desu ka?
Do you have anything other than for your personal use?

いいえ持って いません。
Iie,　motte imasen.
No, I haven't anything.

タバコ や 酒　等　の 禁制品　　をお持ち　です　か。
Tabako ya sake nado no kinseihin o o-mochi[2] desu ka?
Do you have any cigarettes, liquor or other restricted goods

タバコ を少し　　持って います。
Tabako o sukoshi motte imasu.
I have a few cigarettes.

---

[1]See Key to Pronunciation, Alternations of Consonants : pp. 10-11.
[2]See Grammar, Formal Language : pp. 107-108 for the use of honorifics.

フィルム は 何本　お持ち です か。
Fuirumu wa nambon o-mochi[1] desu ka?
How many rolls of film do you have?

二 三 本 だけ 持って います。
Ni-sam-bon dake motte imasu.
I have only a few rolls. (lit., I have two or three rolls.)

滞在 期間 は どの 位　です か。
Taizai kikan wa dono kurai desu ka?
How long is your stay?

二ヵ月　です。
Ni-kagetsu desu.
Two months.

タクシー を 呼んで 下さい。
Takushi o yonde kudasai.
Please call a taxi for me.

TRAVEL BY RAIL

次　の 京都　行き の 汽車 は 何時 です か。
Tsugi no Kyōto yuki no kisha wa nanji desu ka?
What time is the next train for Kyoto?

特別　急行　「鳩」　が 十二時半 に 東京　を 出ま
Tokubetsu kyūkō "Hato" ga jūniji-han ni Tōkyō o dema-
す。全部　指定席　です。
su. Zembu shiteiseki desu.
The special express "Pigeon" leaves Tokyo at 12:30. All seats
are reserved.

いつ 着きます　か。
Itsu tsukimasu ka?
When does it arrive there?

---

[1] See Grammar, Formal Language: pp. 107-108 for the use of honorifics.

ちょうど八時 に 着きます。 七時間 半 かかります。
Chōdo hachiji ni tsukimasu. Shichijikan-han kakarimasu.
It arrives there exactly at eight o'clock. It takes seven and a half hours.

往復 いくらです か。
Ōfuku ikura desu ka?
How much is the round-trip fare?

二千 四 百 円 です。
Nisen yon-hyaku en desu.
It is 2,400 yen.

一等	特別二等	二等
Ittō.	**Tokubetsu nitō.**	**Nitō.**
First class.	*Special second class.*	*Second class.*

片道
Katamichi.
One way.

汽車 が 出発 します。 皆様 御 乗車 願い
Kisha ga shuppatsu shimasu.   Minasama go-jōsha[1] negai
ます。
masu.
The train is leaving. All aboard please.

食堂車 は どこ です か。
Shokudōsha wa doko desu ka?
Where is the dining car?

三輛目 です。
Sanryō-me desu.
It is the third car.

展望車 は どこ です か。
Tembōsha wa doko desu ka?
Where is the observation car?

---

[1]See Grammar, Formal Language: pp. 107-108 for the use of honorifics.

最終車　　です。
Saishūsha desu.
It is the last car.

日本　の　汽車　旅行　には　駅弁　が　あります。駅　で
Nippon no kisha ryokō niwa ekiben ga arimasu. Eki de
折詰　を買って　行く　先々　　の　味を楽しみ　　ながら
orizume o katte, yuku sakizaki no aji o tanoshimi nagara
旅行　をします。
ryokō o shimasu.
*There is **ekiben** (station luncheon) for train travel in Japan.*
***Orizume** (food packed in a chip box) is available at various*
stations; railway passengers in Japan buy it and sample the
taste of many different regional specialities while traveling.

GETTING AROUND TOWN

タクシー
Takushii!
Taxi!

丸の内　　　　　ホテル　へ願います。
Marunouchi Hoteru e negaimasu.
Take me to Marunouchi Hotel, please.

高島屋　　　　　へ　願います。
Takashimaya e negaimasu.
Take me to Takashimaya (Department Store), please.

いくら　です　か。
Ikura desu ka?
How much is it?

メーターに　出て　います。
Mētā　ni dete imasu.
(The fare) is shown on the meter.

Kokuden (Government-operated trains)

上野　一　枚。
Ueno, ichi-mai.
(Give me) one ticket for Ueno.

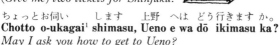

新宿　　　二 枚。
Shinjuku, ni-mai.
(Give me) two tickets for Shinjuku.

ちょっとお伺い　　　します　　上野　へは　どう行きますか。
Chotto o-ukagai[1] shimasu, Ueno e wa dō ikimasu ka?
May I ask you how to get to Ueno?

三番線　　　から　山手線　　　で　五つ目　　　です。上野
Samban-sen kara Yamate-sen de itsutsu-me desu. Ueno
駅　から 十分　　　位　　歩いて上野　公園　を抜ける と 国
Eki kara juppun gurai aruite Ueno Kōen o nukeru to Koku
立　博物館　　　　　科学　博物館　　　　美術館　
ritsu Hakubutsukan, Kagaku Hakubutsukan, Bijutsukan,
動物園　　など が あります。
Dōbutsuen nado ga arimasu.
It is the fifth station on the Yamate line on platform No. 3.
If you walk for ten minutes from Ueno Station through
Ueno Park, you will find the National Museum, the Science
Museum, the Art Gallery, the Zoological Garden, etc.

恐れ　入ります 新宿　　　へは　どう行きますか。
Osore irimasu, Shinjuku e wa dō ikimasu ka?
Excuse me, can you tell me the way to Shinjuku?

一番線　　　で 中央線　　　に お乗りなさい。十五分　　　です。
Ichiban-sen de Chūō-sen ni o-norinasai.[1] Jūgo-fun desu.
Take the Chuo line on platform No. 1. It takes fifteen
minutes.

御覧　の ように(前後　の 駅 その 他)全部　日本語　と
Goran no yōni, (zengo no eki sono ta) zembu Nihongo to
ローマ字で 書いてあります。だから　迷う　心配　　が
Rōmaji de kaite arimasu. Dakara mayou shimpai ga
ありません。
arimasen.
As you see, everything is written both in Japanese and
Romanization, including the preceding and the following
stations. Therefore, you need not worry about getting lost.

---

[1]See Grammar, Formal Language: pp. 107-108 for the use of honorifics.

Chikatetsu (Subway)

国会　議事堂 へ行きたいの です。
Kokkai Gijidō e ikitai　no desu.
I would like to go to the National Diet.

地下鉄　で 五分　です。
Chikatetsu de go-fun desu.
It is five minutes by subway.

いくら です か。
Ikura desu ka?
How much is it?

二十五　円 です。
Nijū-go en desu.
It is twenty-five yen.

とても　綺麗な 地下鉄　ですね。ピンク 色 です。
Totemo kireina chikatetsu desu nē. Pinku iro desu.
It is a very beautiful subway, isn't it? It is pink.

はいそうです。五年　ばかり 前　に 出来ました。　古い　ほう
Hai, sōdesu. Go-nen bakari mae ni dekimashita. Furui hō
は ニューヨークの と 似ています。
wa New York no to nite imasu.
Yes, it is. It was built only five years ago. The old one resembles that of New York.

Toden or Shiden[1] (Streetcars)

魚市場　を見たいの です。
Uo-ichiba o mitai no desu.
I would like to see the fish market.

---

[1]Streetcars in the city of Tokyo are called **toden;** in other cities they are called **shiden.**

それ は 築地 です。四番 の 電車 に 乗って終点
Sore wa Tsukiji desu. Yo-ban no densha ni notte shūten
で 降りると すぐ です。朝 早い 方 が 面白い です。
de oriru to sugu desu. Asa hayai hō ga omoshiroi desu.
It is at Tsukiji. Take the No. 4 streetcar and get off at the terminal. It is near there. It is interesting early in the morning.

恐れ 入ります、歌舞伎座 へ行く 道 を 教えて 下さい。
Osore irimasu, Kabukiza e yuku michi o oshiete kudasai.
Excuse me, please show me the way to the Kabukiza.

真直ぐ 三丁 程 行って右側 です。
Massugu san-chō hodo itte migi-gawa desu.
Go straight ahead for about three blocks. You will find it on the right side.

ちょっとお伺い します, 明治 神宮 へは どの 電車
Chotto o-ukagai[1] shimasu, Meiji Jingū e wa dono densha
が 行きます か。
ga ikimasu ka?
Pardon me, may I ask you what streetcar goes to Meiji Shrine?

十番 の 電車 に 乗って明治 神宮 前 で 降りなさい。
Jū-ban no densha ni notte Meiji Jingū Mae de orinasai.
三十分 かかります。
Sanjuppun kakarimasu.
Take No. 10 streetcar and get off at Meiji Jingu Mae. It takes thirty minutes.

どうもありがとうございます。
Dōmo arigatō gozaimasu.
Thank you very much.

往復 を 下さい。 いくら です か。
Ōfuku o kudasai. Ikura desu ka?
Give me a round-trip ticket. How much is it?

---

[1]See Grammar, Formal Language: pp. 107-108 for the use of honorifics.

二十五　円　です。
Nijū-go en desu.
It is twenty-five yen.

Buses

回数券　を下さい。
Kaisūken o kudasai.
Give me a book of tickets.

百　　円　です。
Hyaku en desu.
It is one hundred yen.

渋谷　へ来たら教えて　下さい。
Shibuya e kitara oshiete kudasai.
Please let me know when we get to Shibuya.

この　バス　は　何時　迄　ありますか。
Kono basu wa nan-ji made arimasu ka?
How late does this bus operate?

九時　半　迄　です。
Kuji-han[1] made desu.
(It is) until half past nine.

AT THE HOTEL

風呂　付　の　個室　を願います。
Furo-tsuki no koshitsu o negaimasu.
May I have a single room with bath.

いつ　迄　お泊まり　です　か。
Itsu made o-tomari[2] desu ka?
How long are you going to stay?

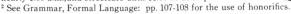

---

[1] Buses in Japan usually stop early in the evening. Trains operate until nearly 1:00 a.m., and streetcars until 11:00 or 11:30 p.m.

[2] See Grammar, Formal Language: pp. 107-108 for the use of honorifics.

一週間　程　です。
Isshūkan hodo desu.
I will stay here about a week.

この　部屋　は　いくらです　か。
Kono heya wa ikura desu ka?
What is the price of this room?

一泊　千　四百　　円　です　が，十パーセント　の　チツプ
Ippaku sen yon-hyaku en desu ga, jup-pāsento no chippu
と　更に　十パーセント　の　税金　を　頂きます　　から　千
to sarani jup-pāsento no zeikin o itadakimasu kara sen
七百　　円　に　なります。
nana-hyaku en ni narimasu.
It is 1,400 yen a day, but a ten percent tip and another ten percent tax should be added. Therefore, it adds up to 1,700 yen a day.

食事　付　です　か。
Shokuji-tsuki desu ka?
Are meals included?

いいえ，別　勘定　です。
Iie, betsu kanjō desu.
No, they are presented in a separate bill.

朝飯　は　何時　です　か。
Asahan wa nan-ji desu ka?
What time is breakfast served?

七時　　から　九時半　迄　です。
Shichiji kara kuji-han made desu.
It is from seven o'clock to half past nine.

では　八時　半　に　起して　下さい。
Dewa, hachiji-han ni okoshite kudasai.
Then, please wake me up at half past eight.

貴重品　をお預り　　しましようか。
Kichōhin o o-azukari[1] shimashō ka?
Shall we keep your valuables (in the safe)?

はい, お願い　します。
Hai, onegai shimasu.
Yes, please do so.

部屋　の　鍵　をお持ち　下さい。
Heya no kagi o o-mochi[1] kudasai.
Please take a key to your room.

食堂　　　は　どこ　です　か。
Shokudō wa doko desu ka?
Where is the dining room?

一階　です。
Ikkai desu.
It is on the first floor.

娯楽　室　　は　どこ　です　か。
Goraku-shitsu wa doko desu ka?
Where is the recreation room?

やはり　一階　です。
Yahari ikkai desu.
It is also on the first floor.

今日　昼　に　立ちます。　　お勘定　　を願います。
Kyō hiru ni tachimasu. O-kanjō[1] o negaimasu.
I am leaving at noon today. Please give me (my) bill.

タクシー　を　呼んで　下さい。
Takushii o yonde kudasai.
Please call a taxi.

---

[1]See Grammar, Formal Language: pp. 107-108 for the use of honorifics.

AT THE RYOKAN (Japanese-Style Inn)

部屋 が あります か。
Heya ga arimasu ka?
Is there a (vacant) room?

はい、ございます。 いつ 迄　お泊まり です か。
Hai, gozaimasu. Itsu made o-tomari[1] desu ka?
Yes, there is.　How long do you intend to stay?

四晩　です。
Yo-ban desu.
Four nights.

庭 に 面した　部屋 が ございます。 御覧 に 入れましょ
Niwa ni menshita heya ga gozaimasu. Goran ni iremashō
か。
ka?
There is a room which faces the garden. Would you like to have a look? (lit., Shall I show you [it]?)

はい、お願い します。
Hai, onegai shimasu.
Yes, please do.

靴　をお脱ぎ に なって 下さい，　こちら にスリッパ が
Kutsu o o-nugi[1] ni natte kudasai, kochira ni surippa ga
ございます。 どうぞこちら　へ。
gozaimasu. Dōzo kochira e.
Please take your shoes off; here are slippers. Please come this way.

お庭　が とても 綺麗 です ね。
O-niwa[1] ga totemo kirei desu nē.
The garden is very beautiful, isn't it?

こちら　で ございます。
Kochira de gozaimasu.
Here is your room.

---

[1]See Grammar, Formal Language: pp. 107-108 for the use of honorifics.

気持 が 良さそうです ね。
Kimochi ga yosasō desu nē.
It seems pleasant, doesn't it?

いくら です か。
Ikura desu ka?
How much is it?

一泊 二食 付 で二千 円 です。それから チップ
Ippaku ni-shoku-tsuki de ni-sen en desu. Sorekara chippu
と 税金 を十パーセント づつ 頂戴 します から 二千
to zeikin o jup-pāsento zutsu chōdai shimasu kara nisen
四百 二十 円 に なります。
yon-hyaku nijū en ni narimasu.
*It is 2,000 yen a day including two meals (dinner and break-
fast).   And a ten percent tip for each (day) and tax will
be charged. These make a total of 2,420 yen a day.*

記帳 をお願い します。
Kichō o onegai shimasu.
Please register.

貴重品 を帳場 へお預け に なります か。
Kichōhin o chōba e o-azuke[1] ni narimasu ka?
Would you like the desk to keep your valuables (for you)?

お夕食 は 何時 に上がります か。 女中 が 持って
O-yūshoku wa nan-ji ni agarimasu ka?   Jochū ga motte
伺います。
ukagaimasu.
*At what time will you have dinner? A maid will bring it
to you.*

七時 に 願います。
Shichiji ni negaimasu.
At seven o'clock, please.

何 を召し上がります か。
Nani o meshiagarimasu ka?
What would you like to have (for dinner)?

---

[1]See Grammar, Formal Language: pp. 107-108 for the use of honorifics.

何か　和食　が　いいです。
Nanika washoku ga iidesu.
I would like to have some Japanese food.

そうですね。じゃすき焼　に　なさいます　か。
Sōdesu ne. Ja, sukiyaki ni nasaimasuka?
Let me see. Well, how about sukiyaki?

はい　結構　です。
Hai, kekkō desu.
Yes, please.

お風呂[1]　は　いつ　お入り[1]　に　なります　か。
O-furo[1] wa itsu o-hairi[1] ni narimasu ka?
When will you take a bath?

食事　前　六時　に　しましょう。
Shokuji mae rokuji ni shimashō.
Let me take it before dinner at six o'clock.

では　六時　に　御案内[1]　致します。
Dewa rokuji ni go-annai[1] itashimasu.
Then I will take you there at six o'clock.

ここ　に　たんぜんが　ございます　から　どうぞ。
Koko ni tanzen ga gozaimasu kara dōzo.
Here is a tanzen (padded bathrobe); please (wear it).

何時　に　床　を　おとり[1]　致しましょうか。
Nanji ni toko o o-tori[1] itasimashō ka?
At what time shall I prepare the bed?

だいぶ　疲れました　ので　はやめ　に　お願い　します。
Daibu tsukaremashita no de, hayame ni onegai shimasu.
Since I am pretty tired, please do it early.

では，　十時に　どうですか。
Dewa, jūji ni dōdesu ka?
Well, how about (at) ten o'clock?

---

[1]See Grammar, Formal Language: pp. 107-108 for the use of honorifics.

もう少し　後　でも　かまいません。
Mō sukoshi ato demo kamaimasen.
Even if it is a little later, it is still all right.

この　シャツ　をプレス　して　下さい。
Kono shatsu o puresu shite kudasai.
Please press this shirt.

はい, かしこまりました。
Hai, kashikomarimashita.
Yes, all right, sir.

明日　立ちます　から, お勘定　を　願います。
Ashita tachimasu kara, o-kanjō[1] o negaimasu.
Since I am leaving tomorrow, please have a bill ready.

大変　寛ぎました。
Taihen kutsurogimashita.
I felt so comfortable here.

THE SIDEWALK RESTAURANT

ビールを二本　お願い　します。
Biiru o ni-hon onegai shimasu.
Bring me two bottles of beer, please.

何印　が　いいですか。
Nani-jirushi[2] ga ii desu ka?
What brand do you want?

「きりん」が　いいです。
"Kirin" ga ii desu.
I like "Kirin" (giraffe) brand.

はい, かしこまりました。
Hai, kashikomarimashita.
Yes, all right, sir.

---

[1]See Grammar, Formal Language: pp. 107-108 for the use of honorifics.
[2]See Key to Pronunciation, Alternations of Consonants: pp. 10-11

鰻丼　　　　　　　を 願います。
Unagi-domburi o negaimasu.
*I would like to have an **unagi-domburi** (eel on rice).*

残念　です が、只今　　切れて おります。親子丼
Zannen desu ga, tadaima kirete orimasu. Oyako-domburi
は どうです か。
wa dō desu ka?
*It's too bad, we are out of it now. How about an **oyako-domburi** (bowl of rice covered with chicken, egg and vegetables)?*

結構　です。
Kekkō desu.
It is all right.

お勘定　願います。
O-kanjō[1] negaimasu.
Check, please.

ここ に 置きます から、お帰り　がけ にカウンターでお支
Koko ni okimasu kara, o-kaeri[1] gake ni kauntā de o-shi
払い 下さい。
harai[1] kudasai.
I will leave the bill here ; please pay it at the counter when you leave.

DINING OUT

てんぷら をお願い します。
Tempura o onegai shimasu.
May we have tempura?

幾人　様　です か。
Ikunin sama desu ka?
How many (persons are there in the party)?

四人　です。
Yo-nin desu.
Four, please.

[1]See Grammar, Formal Language: pp. 107-108 for the use of honorifics.

では こちら へどうぞ。
Dewa kochira e dōzo.
Then come this way, please.

お食事　　前　に お酒　を上がります か。
O-shokuji[1] mae ni o-sake[1] o agarimasu ka?
*Would you like to have some **sake** (rice wine) before dinner?*

はい, 少し　　お願い します。
Hai, sukoshi onegai shimasu.
Yes, a little please.

そうですね。じゃ二本　おつけ しましょう。
Sōdesu nē. Jā, ni-hon otsuke shimashō.
Let me see. Then I will bring you two bottles.

大変　　おいしいです。
Taihen oishii desu.
This is very delicious.

御飯　をおつけ しましょうか。
Gohan o o-tsuke[1] shimashō ka?
Shall I serve you rice?

はい, お願い します。
Hai, onegai shimasu.
Yes, please do so.

お箸　　は 食べにくい でしようから フォークをお持ち しま
O-hashi[1] wa tabenikui deshō kara, fōku o o-mochi[1] shima
しょうか。
shō ka?
*As it seems to be difficult to eat with chopsticks, shall I bring
you a fork?*

いいえ, かまいません。
Iie, kamaimasen.
No, it doesn't matter.

---

[1]See Grammar, Formal Language: pp. 107-108 for the use of honorifics.

お茶 をもう少し 頂けます か。
O-cha[1] o mō sukoshi itadakemasu ka?
May I have some more tea?

はい、かしこまりました。 只今 お持ち 致します。
Hai, kashikomarimashita. Tadaima o-mochi[1] itashimasu.
Yes, all right, sir. I will bring it now.

日本 の お茶 が お好き です か。
Nippon no o-cha[1] ga o-suki[1] desu ka?
Do you like Japanese tea?

はい、とても 好き です。
Hai, totemo suki desu.
Yes, I like it very much.

和食 も お好き です か。
Wa-shoku mo o-suki[1] desu ka?
Do you also like Japanese food?

はい、大好き です。
Hai, dai-suki desu.
Yes, I like it very much.

お勘定 をお願い します。
O-kanjō[1] o onegai shimasu.
Give me the bill, please.

はい、少々 お待ち 下さい。
Hai, shōshō o-machi[1] kudasai.
Yes, please wait just a moment.

大変 お待たせ 致しました。 どうもありがとうございます。
Taihen o-matase[1] itashimashita. Dōmo arigato gozaimasu.
Sorry to keep you waiting. Thank you very much.

NATIVE DISHES

Sukiyaki : Casserole of beef, onions, mixed vegetables, bean
curd, etc.,cooked with soy-sauce and sugar in a chafing
dish.

---

[1]See Grammar, Formal Language: pp. 107-108 for the use of honorifics.

Tempura : Fish and vegetables in batter, fried in deep oil.

Chawan-mushi : Custard-like dish of thick soup containing mushrooms, nuts, egg, bamboo sprouts, Japanese parsley, etc. (usually the vegetable in season).

Misoshiru : Bean-paste soup (usually eaten for breakfast).

Sashimi : Raw tuna, sea-bream, octopus, cuttlefish, served with soy-sauce and Japanese horse-radish.

Norimaki : Cold rice rolled into a cylindrical form, wrapped in seaweed and containing cooked egg, vegetable, etc. (for travel, picnics).

Inarizushi : Triangular fried bean-curd jacket, filled with rice, mushrooms, bamboo sprouts, etc.

Sushi : Cold rice, rolled into a cylindrical form, topped with Japanese horse-radish and raw fish.

The names of foreign dishes are often used in their adapted Japanese form :

katsuretsu	*(pork) cutlet*
sutēki	*steak*
omuretsu	*omelet*
appuru pai	*apple pie*
dezāto	*dessert*
kōhii	*coffee*
aisu kurimu	*ice cream*
shichū	*stew*
karē raisu	*curry rice*
sūpu	*soup*
jūsu	*bottled fruit-flavored drinks (juice)*

SIGHTSEEING AND ENTERTAINMENT

東京　タワーへどう行きますか。
Tōkyō Tawā e dō ikimasu ka?
What is the way to the Tokyo Tower?
(lit., *How to go to the Tokyo Tower?*)

そこ から バス で すぐ です。
Soko kara basu de sugu desu.
It is very near by bus.

街　　を見物　　　したいの です が どうしたらいいでしょうか。
Machi o kembutsu shitai no desu ga dōshitara iideshō　ka?
What is the best way to go sightseeing in the city?
(*lit., I would like to have sightseeing in the city, so how can I do?*)

観光　　バス が 一番　　　よろしい でしょう。「鳩」 バス が
Kankō basu ga ichiban yoroshii deshō. "Hato" basu ga
東京　駅 の 前　 から 出て います。確か　　　四時間　と
Tokyo Eki no mae kara dete imasu. Tashika yojikan to
八時間　　　コースが あったと 思います。　お問合せ　に
hachijikan kōsu ga atta to omoimasu. O-toiawase[1] ni
なれば よろしいでしょう。交通公社　で 全国　　　の 旅行
nareba yoroshii deshō. Kōtsūkōsha[2] de zenkoku no ryokō
計画　を立てて くれます。
keikaku o tatete kuremasu.

A sightseeing bus will be best. A "Pigeon" bus leaves from (the plaza) in front of Tokyo Station. I think there are perhaps four-hour and eight-hour tours (courses). I would suggest you inquire about them there. The Japan Travel Bureau is available for sightseeing plans throughout the country.

どうもありがとうございます。
Dōmo arigatō gozaimasu.
Thank you very much.

どう致しまして。
Dō itashimashite.
You are welcome.

---

[1] See Grammar, Formal Language: pp. 107-108 for the use of honorifics.
[2] The Japanese Travel Bureau, whose headquarters are at Marunouchi, Tokyo, has branch offices in main cities throughout Japan. It helps tourists in various ways, particularly in planning sightseeing trips.

Kabuki[1]

再来週　　の　水曜日　夜の部　　　三枚　　　あります　か。
Saraishū no Sui-yobi yoru-no-bu sam-mai arimasu ka?
Can you give me three tickets for the evening performance on Wednesday, a week after next?

はい　ございます。
Hai, gozaimasu.
Yes, we can (lit., we have).

どの　席　　が　よいです　か。
Dono seki ga yoi desu ka?
What seats are good (do you recommend me)?

そうですね。この辺　は　どうですか。よく　御覧　に　なれ
Sōdesu ne. Konohen wa dō desu ka? Yoku goran ni nare
ます。二等席です。
masu.[2] Nitō seki desu.
Let me see.　How about these seats? (lit.,How about around here?)　You can see very well.　These are second class.

結構　です。
Kekkō desu.
That's fine.

Bunraku[3]

文楽　　を見たいの　です。
Bunraku o mitai no desu.
I would like to see a Bunraku.

---

[1] Popular classical dance and drama of Japan dates from the seventeenth century.　It is a blend of the graphic arts with music, dance, action and literature.　The meaning is presented by word and song, sensory perception by the interpretive gestures, and emotional impact by the accompanying music.

[2] See Grammar, Formal Language: pp. 107-108 for the use of honorifics.

[3] The puppet theatre dates from the sixteenth century.　Its historical development is invariably interwoven with that of Kabuki.　A puppet is manipulated by three men: the head puppeteer holds the doll by the back to operate the right hand and eyebrows; a second man operates the left hand; and a third man operates the feet of male dolls and the skirts of female dolls which gives the impression of walking and leg movements.

おあいにく様 です が 只今 東京 興行 をして いません。
Oainikusama desu ga tadaima Tōkyō kōgyō o shite imasen.
大阪 です。これ は 関西 のお芝居 ですから やはり
Osaka desu. Kore wa Kansai no o-shibai[1] desu kara yahari
あちら で 御覧 になって頂く わけ です ね。
achira de goran ni natte itadaku wake desu nē.
I am very sorry but there is no performance in Tokyo now.
It is in Osaka. Since this is a show of **Kansai** (*Kyoto-Osaka-*
Kobe area), *you should see it there after all.*

Nō[2]

能 を見たいの です。
Nō o mitai no desu.
I would like to see a Nō

明日 の 席 が まだ ございます。何 枚 御入用 です
Ashita no seki ga mada gozaimasu. Nan-mai go-iriyō[1] desu
か。
ka?
Seats for tomorrow are still available. How many would
you like to have?

四 枚 下さい。
Yo-mai kudasai.
Give me four.

場所 は どこ です か。
Basho wa doko desu ka?
Where does it play?

---

[1] See Grammar, Formal Language: pp. 107-108 for the use of honorifics.
[2] Classical lyric drama of Japan began in the fourteenth century. The
program includes folk and other traditional dancing, religious entertain-
ments, priests' moral instructions, and the play of elegant nobles. The
language is extremely elaborate and polite. Short comic interludes,
called **Kyōgen,** occur between the more dramatic **Nō** plays.

能楽堂　　　です。水道橋　　　迄　　　国電　　　　で いらっしゃれば
Nōgakudō desu. Suidōbashi made Kokuden de irasshareba
すぐ 分ります。
sugu wakarimasu.
It is at Nogakudo. If you go to Suidobashi by Kokuden you
can find it easily.

Sumō Wrestling

相撲　 を見られますか。
Sumō o miraremasuka。
Can I see Sumo matches?

はい、只今　　　夏場所　　　開催中　　 です。
Hai, tadaima natubasho kaisaichū desu.
Yes, the summer matches are on now.

そうですか。じゃこの 土曜日　 のを二枚　　下さい。
Sōdesu ka. Jā, kono Do-yōbi no o ni-mai kudasai.
Is that so? Well, give me two tickets for this coming Saturday.

どの　席　をお取り しましょうか。　　桟敷　が まだ　少々
Dono seki o o-tori[1] shimashō ka?　Sajiki ga mada shōshō
ございます。
gozaimasu.
What seats shall I reserve? We still have a few box seats.

では　それを願います。
Dewa sore o negaimasu.
Then please reserve them.

PHOTOGRAPHY

恐れ　入りますが、ちょっと写真　　を取らせて 頂けます
Osore irimasu ga, chotto shashin o torasete itadakemasu
か。
ka?
Excuse me, may I trouble you to take your picture?

---

[1]See Grammar, Formal Language: pp. 107-108 for the use of honorifics.

はい, どうぞ。
Hai, dōzo.
Yes, please.

では そこ へ お立ち に なって 下さい。 この 着物 は
Dewa soko e o-tachi ni natte kudasai. Kono kimono wa
大変 綺麗 です ね。
taihen kirei desu nē.
Then please stand there. This kimono is very beautiful.

大変 失礼 しました。
Taihen shitsurei shimashita.
Thank you very much for your trouble.
(lit., I was very impolite to you.)

この フィルム を現像 と 焼付 して 下さい。
Kono fuirumu o genzō to yakitsuke shite kudasai.
Please develop and print this roll of film.

はい かしこまりました。 来週 の 火曜日 に 出来ます。
Hai, kashikomarimashita. Rai-shū no Ka-yōbi ni dekimasu.
Yes, all right, sir. This will be ready next Tuesday.

カラーフィルム が あります か。
Karā fuirumu ga arimasu ka?
Do you have color film?

はい「富士カラー」が ございます。
Hai, "Fujicolor" ga gozaimasu.
Yes, we have "Fujicolor."

じゃ三 本 下さい。
Jā, sam-bon kudasai.
Well, give me three rolls, please.

中 に 使い方 が 英語 と 日本語 で 書いてあります。
Naka ni tsukaikata ga Eigo to Nihongo de kaite arimasu.
You will find instructions on the use of this film, both in English and Japanese, inside.

フラッシ　バルブ　も　あります　か。
Furasshi barubu mo arimasu ka?
Do you also have flashbulbs?

はい　ございます。　おいくつ¹　御入用¹　です　か。
Hai, gozaimasu. O-ikutsu¹ go-iriyō¹ desu ka?
Yes, we have. How many do you need?

半ダース　下さい。
Han-dāsu kudasai.
Give me a half a dozen.

この　写真　を引き延ばし　して　下さい。
Kono shashin o hikinobashi shite kudasai.
Please enlarge this picture.

いつ　出来ますか。
Itsu dekimasu ka?
When will they be ready?

明後日　の　午後　に　出来ます。
Asatte no gogo ni dekimasu.
They will be ready the day after tomorrow in the afternoon.

SHOPPING

デパートは　どこ　です　か。
Depāto wa doko desu ka?
Where are the department stores?

地下鉄　　で　日本橋　　へ出なさい。三越　　と
chikatetsu de Nihonbashi e denasai. Mitsukoshi to
白木屋　と　高島屋　　が　あります。または　やはり
Shirokiya to Takashimaya ga arimasu. Matawa yahari
地下鉄　で　銀座　へ出ると　松屋　と三越　と
chikatetsu de Ginza e deruto Matsuya to Mitsukoshi to
松阪屋　が　あります。
Matsuzakaya ga arimasu.
Take the subway to Nihonbashi to the Mitsukoshi, Shirokiya and Takashimaya (Department Stores). Or you can go to Ginza by subway to the Matsuya, Mitsukoshi and Matsuzakaya (Department Stores).

¹See Grammar, Formal Language: pp. 107-108 for the use of honorifics.

この　人形　は　いくらです　か。
Kono ningyō wa ikura desu ka?
How much is this doll?

二千六百　　　　　円　です。
Nisen roppyaku en desu.
It is 2,600 yen.

この　着物　は　いくらです　か。草履　は。
Kono kimono wa ikura desu ka? Zōri wa?
How much is this kimono? How about these zōri (sandals for kimono)?

着物　は　五千　八百　　　　円　で　草履　は　千　二百　　　円
Kimono wa gosen happyaku en de, zōri wa sen ni-hyaku en
です。
desu.
The kimono is 5,800 yen and the zōri are 1,200 yen.

この　ブロケイドは　いくらですか。
Kono brokēdo wa ikura desu ka?
How much is this brocade material?

一メートル　千　百　　　円　です。
Ichimētoru sen hyaku en desu.
It is 1,100 yen per meter.

この　生地で　もう少し　　淡い　色　が　あります　か。
Kono kiji de mō sukoshi awai iro ga arimasu ka?
Do you have this material in a lighter color?

はい, ございます。空色　　は　いかが　です　か。
Hai, gozaimasu. Sora-iro wa ikaga desu ka?
Yes, we have it. How about light blue?

はい, 結構　です。
Hai, kekkō desu.
Yes, that's good.

この　漆器　は　いくら　です　か。
Kono shikki wa ikura desu ka?
How much is this lacquer ware?

九百　　　円 です。
Kyū-hyaku en desu.
It is 900 yen.

お届け　　しましょうか。
O-todoke[1] shimashō ka?
Shall we send them to you?

はい, お願い します。
Hai, onegai shimasu.
Yes, please do so.

骨董品屋　　は どこ です か。
Kottōhin-ya wa doko desu ka?
Where is a curio shop?

方々 に あります。 高島屋　　　の 地下 にも 確か
Hōbō ni arimasu. Takashimaya no chika nimo tashika
ありました。
arimashita.
There are some at various places. I think there is one in the
basement of Takashimaya Department Store.

タバコ を二つ　下さい。
Tabako o futatsu kudasai.
Give me two packages of cigarettes.

何の　　しるし　が よろしい です か。
Nan-no shirushi ga yoroshii desu ka?
What brand do you like?

「いこい」と「ピース」を一つずつ　　　下さい。
"Ikoi" to "Peace" o hitotsu-zutsu kudasai.
Give me one each of "Ikoi" (repose) and "Peace".

LAUNDRY AND DRY CLEANING

この 背広　 に ボタンをつけて 頂けます　　か。
Kono sebiro ni botan o tsukete itadakemasu ka?
Would you please sew a button on this suit?

---

[1]See Grammar, Formal Language: pp. 107-108 for the use of honorifics.

この　シャツを洗って少し　糊　をつけて　下さい。
Kono shatsu o aratte sukoshi nori o tsukete kudasai.
Please wash this shirt and starch it a little.

この　背広　を急いでドライクリーニングして　ほしい　の　です。
Kono sebiro o isoide dorai kuriiningu shite hoshii no desu.
I want this suit dry-cleaned in a hurry.

いつ　出来ます　か。
Itsu dekimasu ka?
When can you have it ready?

では　明日　の　夕方　でいかが　です　か。
Dewa ashita no yūgata de ikaga desu ka?
Then how about tomorrow evening?

この　ずぼんをプレス　して　下さい。
Kono zubon o puresu shite kudasai.
Please press these trousers.

この　シャツ　の　綻び　を縫って頂けます　か。
Kono shatsu no hokorobi o nutte itadakemasu ka?
Would you please mend a tear in this shirt?

HAIRDRESSERS AND BARBERS

美容院　へ行きたいの　です　が　どこ　か　よい所　を教えて
Biyōin e ikitai no desu ga, doko ka yoi tokoro o oshiete
下さい。
kudasai.
I would like to go to a hairdresser; can you recommend a good one?

髪　をセットしてほしい　の　です。
Kami o setto shite hoshii no desu.
I would like to have my hair set.

もう少し　短かく　して　下さい。
Mō sukoshi mijikaku shite kudasai.
Please cut it shorter.

マニキュア を お願い します。
Manikyua o onegai shimasu.
Please give me a manicure.

床屋 は どこ です か。
Tokoya wa doko desu ka?
Where is a barber?

散髪 して 洗って ほしい の です。
Sampatsu shite aratte hoshii no desu.
I would like to have my hair cut and washed.

もっと 短かく （長く） 刈って 下さい。
Motto mijikaku (nagaku) katte kudasai.
Please cut it short (long).

髭 を 剃って 下さい。
Hige o sotte kudasai.
I would like a shave.

A VISIT TO MR. TANAKA

ご免 下さい。 河合 で ございます。
Gomen kudasai. Kawai de gozaimasu.
Hello. I am (Mr.) Kawai.

御主人[1] 様 は 御在宅[1] でいらっしゃいますか。
Go-shujin[1] sama wa go-zaitaku[1] de irasshaimasu ka?
Is your husband at home?

はい、おります。どうぞお上がり 下さい。
Hai, orimasu. Dōzo o-agari[1] kudasai.
Yes, he is in. Please come in.

よく いらっしゃいました。お茶 をどうぞ。
Yoku irasshaimashita. O-cha o dōzo.
I am very happy to see you. Please have some tea.

皆様 は お変り ございません か。
Minasama wa o-kawari[1] go-zaimasen[1] ka?
Are you all well?

---

[1]See Grammar, Formal Language: pp. 107-108 for the use of honorifics.

はい, お蔭様　　　で 元気　です。
Hai, okagesama de genki desu.
Yes, we are fine, thank you.

EXCHANGING MONEY

為替相場　　は いくらです か。
Kawase-sōba wa ikura desu ka?
How much is the exchange rate?

三百　　　　六十　　円 対 一 ドル です。
Sambyaku ryokujū en tai ichi doru desu.
It is 360 yen to a dollar.

この　旅客用　　小切手 を 現金　に して 下さい。
Kono ryokakuyō-kogitte o genkin ni shite kudasai.
Please cash this traveler's check.

この 一万　　円 札　をくずして 下さい。
Kono ichi-man en satsu o kuzushite kudasai.
Please change this 10,000 yen note.

百　　円を細かく　　して 下さい。
Hyaku en o komakaku shite kudasai.
Please give me small change for 100 yen.

COMMUNICATIONS
Mail and Telegrams[1]

郵便局　　は どこ です か。
Yūbin kyoku wa doko desu ka?
Where is the post office?

何時　迄 開いています か。
Nanji made aite imasu ka?
Until what time is it open?

---

[1] In Japan mail is handled by the Ministry of Postal Service, and telegrams by the Public Telegram and Telephone Corporation. These offices are usually located next to each other.

東京　　中央　郵便局　　　は　一晩中　　開いていますが　二
Tōkyō Chūō Yūbinkyoku wa hitobanjū aite imasu ga, ni-
等局　　は　八時　　迄　　で　特定局　　　は　六時　　迄
tō kyoku wa hachiji made de, tokutei kyoku wa rokuji made
です。
desu.
The Tokyo Central Post Office is open all night, but the second-class post offices are open until eight o'clock and the special post offices are open until six o'clock.

こちら　の　郵便料金　　は。
Kochira no yūbin-ryōkin wa?
What is the postage here?

葉書　　は　五円　で, 手紙　　は　十円　です。速達
Hagaki wa go en de, tegami wa jū en desu. Sokutatsu-
料金　　は　三十　円　で, 書留料金　　　は　四十　円　です。
ryōkin wa sanjū en de, kakitome-ryōkin wa yonjū en desu.
国際　　郵便　の　場合　は　エアレターが　五十　円　で, 航空
Kokusai yūbin no baai wa eā-retā ga gojū en de, kōkū
郵便　は　アメリカ　へは十　グラム　迄　　八十　　　円　です。
yūbin wa Amerika e wa jū guramu made hachijū en desu.
A post card is five yen and a letter is ten yen. The special-delivery fee is thirty yen and the fee for registered mail is forty yen. In the case of international mail, an air letter is fifty yen and air mail to the United States is eighty yen up to ten grams.

では　八十　　円　の　切手　を十枚　　と　エアレターを六枚
Dewa hachijū en no kitte o jū-mai to eā-retā o roku-mai
下さい。
kudasai.
Then give me ten eighty-yen stamps and six air letters.

この　手紙　　を速達　　　で お願い　します。
Kono tegami o sokutatsu de onegai shimasu.
Please send this letter by special delivery.

この　小包　　　は 船便　　で アメリカ 迄　　いくらです
Kono kozutsumi wa funabin de Amerika made ikura desu
か。
ka?
How much is this parcel to the United States by regular mail?

中味　　は 何　です か。
Nakami wa nan desu ka?
What does it contain?

本　と雑誌　です。
Hon to zasshi desu.
Books and magazines.

手紙　　を全部　　ニューヨークへ転送　願います。
Tegami o zembu New York e tensō negaimasu.
Would you please forward all my mail to New York.

電報　　をニューヨークへ打ちたいの です。電報　　用紙　を
Dempō o New York e uchitai no desu. Dempō-yōshi o
ください。
kudasai.
*I want to send a telegram to New York. Give me a blank
for the telegram.*

普通　電報　　です か それとも　遅い　方 です か。
Futsū dempō desu ka, soretomo osoi hō desu ka?
Are you sending it by regular telegram or night letter?

料金　　は。
Ryōkin wa?
What are the rates?

普通　電報　　は 一 語 百　　二十 円 で 遅い 方 は
Futsū dempō wa ichi-go hyaku nijū en de, osoi hō wa
その 半額　　です。
sono hangaku desu.
*The regular telegram rate is 120 yen a word, and the night
letter is half that rate.*

普通　電報　にして　下さい。十二字　でいくらになります
Futsū dempō ni shite kudasai. Jūni-ji de ikura ni narimasu
か？
ka?
By regular telegram, please. How much do twelve words cost?

いつ 着きます　か。
Itsu tsukimasu ka?
When will it get there?

Telephoning

最寄り　の公衆　電話　は　どこ　です　か。
Moyori no kōshū denwa wa doko desu ka?
Where is the nearest public telephone?

もし　もし、秋山　　です　が，松本　　さん　は
Moshi moshi, Akiyama desu ga, Matsumoto san wa
いらっしゃいますか。
irasshaimasu ka?
Hello, this is (Mr.) Akiyama; is Mr. Matsumoto in?

いいえ,只今　出かけて　おります。
Iie, tadaima dekakete orimasu.
No, he is out now.

すぐ　お帰り　に・なります　か。
Sugu o-kaeri[1] ni narimasu ka?
Will he be back soon?

三時　頃　戻る　と存じます。
Sanji koro modoru to zonjimasu.
I think he will be back around three o'clock.

では　お帰り　になりましたら　電話　をお願い　します。
Dewa, o-kaeri[1] ni narimashitara, denwa o onegai shimasu.
Then, when he comes back, I would like him to call me.

---

[1] See Grammar, Formal Language: pp. 107-108 for the use of honorifics.

はい、かしこまりました。
Hai, kashikomarimashita.
Yes, all right, sir.

YOUR HEALTH ABROAD

歯 が 痛みます。 どこ か よい 歯医者 を 教えて 下さい。
Ha ga itamimasu. Dokoka yoi haisha o oshiete kudasai.
I have a toothache. Please direct me to a good dentist somewhere.

気分 が 悪い です。医者 を 呼んで 下さい。
Kibun ga warui desu. Isha o yonde kudasai.
I don't feel well. Please call a doctor for me.

少し 怪我 をしました。
Sukoshi kega o shimashita.
I have had a slight injury.

どこ を 怪我 しました か。
Doko o kega shimashita ka?
Where have you had an injury?

熱 が あります。風邪 を 引いたらしい です。
Netsu ga arimasu. Kaze o hiita rashii desu.
I have a fever. It seems that I have caught a cold.

どこ が 痛いです か。
Doko ga itai desu ka?
Where does it hurt?

頭 と 喉 が 痛いです。背中 も 少し 痛みます。
Atama to nodo ga itai desu. Senaka mo sukoshi itamimasu.
My head and throat ache. My back also aches a little.

薬 屋 は どこ です か。
Kusuri-ya¹ wa doko desu ka?
Where is a drugstore?

---

¹ There is no separation of dispensary from medical practice in Japan. Therefore, one can purchase all medicines at drugstores without doctors' prescriptions.

眼鏡　　が　こわれました。　　新しい　　レンズを入れて　下さい。
Megane ga kowaremashita. Atarashii renzu o irete kudasai.
My glasses are broken. Please put in a new lens.

SPORTS
Suiei (Swimming)

どこ　　で　水着　　に　変えられます　か。
Doko de mizugi ni kaeraremasu ka?
Where can I change into my bathing suit?

タオルを貸して　　もらえます　か。
Taoru o kashite moraemasu ka?
May I rent a towel?

日焼け止め　　ローションは　どこ　で　買えます　か。
Hiyakedome "lotion" wa doko de kaemasu ka?
Where can I buy some sunburn lotion?

陽　が　とても　強い　　です。
Hi ga totemo tsuyoi desu.
The sun is very strong.

Tsuri (Fishing)

釣道具　　　が　ほしい　の　です。
Tsuri-dōgu ga hoshii no desu.
I would like to have some fishing tackle.

どこ　で　舟　を貸します　　か。
Doko de fune o kashimasu ka?
Where can we rent a boat?

Roller and Ice Skating

スケート場は　どこ　です　か。
Skēto-jō wa doko desu ka?
Where is a skating rink?

入場料　　は　いくら　です　か。
Nyūjō-ryō wa ikura desu ka?
What is the admission fee?

スケート靴　は　いくらで　貸します　か。
Skēto-gutsu[1] wa ikura de kashimasu ka?
What is the charge for skates?

何時　迄　開いています　か。
Nan-ji made aite imasu ka?
Until what time is it open?

Yakyū (Baseball)

六大学　　　　野球　の　試合を見に　行きましょう。
Roku-daigaku yakyū no shiai o mini ikimashō.
Let's go to see a six-team intercollegiate baseball game.

今　どの　チーム　の　試合　です　か。
Ima dono chiimu no shiai desu ka?
What teams are playing now?

慶応　と　早稲田　です。
Keiō to Waseda desu.
They are Keiō and Waseda.

スコア　は　何　です　か。
Sukoa wa nan desu ka?
What is the score?

Tennis

テニス　コートは　いくらで　借りられます　か。
Tenisu kōto wa ikura de kariraremasu ka?
What is the charge for the use of a tennis court?

ラケット　を貸して　下さい。
Raketto o kashite kudasai.
Lend me a racket.

球　　を一缶　　下さい。
Tama o hito-kan kudasai.
Give me a can of balls.

---

[1]See Key to Pronunciation, Alternations of Consonants : pp. 10-11.

更衣室　　は　どこ　です　か。
Kōishitsu wa doko desu ka?
Where is the locker room?

CONDUCTING BUSINESS

外人登録証　　　を　申込みたい　　の　です。
Gaijin-tōroku-shō o mōshikomitai no desu.
I wish to apply for an alien registration card.

いつ　出来ます　　か。
Itsu dekimasu ka?
When will it be ready?

いつ　迄　　有効　です　か。
Itsu made yūkō desu ka?
For how long a period is my card valid?

引越したら　　どうします　　か。
Hikkoshitara dō shimasu ka?
If I move from here, what must I do?

繊維会社　　　に　交渉　　したいの　です。
Sen-i-gaisha[1] ni kōshō shitai no desu.
I would like to contact a textile firm.

どこ　がよい　です　か。
Doko ga yoi desu ka?
Where would you recommend?

市場　を視察　　に　来ました。
Shijō o shisatsu ni kimashita.
I have come here to survey the market.

どこ　で会社　の　信用調査　　が　出来ます　か。
Doko de kaisha no shinyō-chōsa ga dekimasu ka?
Where can I check on the firm's credit rating?

---

[1]See Key to Pronunciation, Alternations of Consonants: pp. 10-11.

お宅 の 工場 は どの 程度 の 規模 です か。
O-taku[1] no kōjō wa dono teido no kibo desu ka?
What is the size (lit., scale) of your factory?

幾人 従業員 が います か。
Iku-nin jūgyōin ga imasu ka?
How many people do you employ?
(lit., *How many employees are there?*)

資本 は どれ 程 です か。
Shihon wa dore hodo desu ka?
What is your capital?

工場 を 視察 したいの です が。
Kōjō o shisatsu shitai no desu ga.
May I inspect your factory?

銀行 の 信用照会状 を 頂けます か。
Ginkō no shinyō-shōkaijō o itadakemasu ka?
May I have your bank references?

商品 には ドル で お支払い します。
Shōhin niwa doru de o-shiharai[1] shimasu.
I will pay in dollars for the goods.

いつ 出荷 願えます か。
Itsu shukka negaemasu ka?
When can you ship the merchandise?

---

[1] See Grammar, Formal Language : pp. 107-108 for the use of honorifics.

ENGLISH COGNATES IN JAPANESE

For the sake of convenience, the following is a list of nouns borrowed directly from English and used in daily conversation in Japanese. You can use them either in the Japanese or English form :

eā-reta	air letter	**kurabu**	club
apāto	apartment *or* apartment house	**kurasu**	class
		kyabarē	cabaret
basu	bus	**kyabin**	cabin
batā	butter	**mafurā**	muffler
bēkon	bacon	**māmarēdo**	marmalade
beru	bell	**manikyua**	manicure
biiru	beer	**massāji**	massage
botan	button	**matchi**	match
burausu	blouse	**menyū**	menu
burōchi	brooch	**merodē**	melody
chiimu	team	**mētoru**	meter
chiizu	cheese	**mētā** (for taxi)	meter
chippu	tip	**miruku**	milk
dekki	deck	**misairu**	missile
depāto	department (store)	**naifu**	knife
		nekutai	necktie
doā	door	**panfuretto**	pamphlet
dorai kuriiningu	dry cleaning	**parasoru**	parasol
doru	dollar	**pāsento**	percent
enerugii	energy	**pasu**	pass (examination; commutation ticket)
erebētā	elevator		
esukarētā	escalator		
fōku	fork	**pasupōto**	passport
fuirumu	film	**pedaru**	pedal
furasshi barubu	flashbulb	**pēji**	page
garasu	glass	**pikunikku**	picnic
hamu	ham	**pinku**	pink
hoteru	hotel	**pisutoru**	pistol
kakuteru	cocktail	**pondo**	pound
karā fuirumu	color film	**puresu**	press
katarogu	catalog	**puremiamu**	premium
kāten	curtain	**purezento**	present
kauntā	counter	**rajio**	radio
kōhii	coffee	**raketto**	racket
koppu	cup	**rampu**	lamp
kōsu	course	**resutoran**	restaurant
kūpon	coupon	**renzu**	lens

rizumu	rhythm	**sūtsu**	suits
roketto	rocket		(for women)
sābisu	service	**sūtsu-kēsu**	suitcase
sampuru	sample	**sutokkingu**	stockings
sandoitchi	sandwiches	**tabako**	tobacco
setto	set		(cigarettes)
	(for hairdressing)	**taipuraitā**	typewriter
shatsu	shirt	**takushii**	taxi
shawā (of bath)	shower	**taoru**	towel
sukāto	skirt	**tawā**	tower
sukoa	score	**tēburu**	table
supōtsu	sports	**terebi**	television
spun	spoon	**tenisu-kōto**	tennis court
surippa	slipper	**torakku**	truck
sutoraiki	strike	**toranjisutā**	transistor

OUTLINE OF JAPANESE GRAMMAR

THE NOUN

1. The number and variety of suffixes by means of which a noun can be enlarged is so limited in Japanese that it is more accurate to say that, generally, the Japanese noun is not enlarged by means of suffixes.

2. Thus, the idea of plurality which we find expressed, primarily by means of *-s* in English (*hand-s, cat-s, house-s*) is usually left unexpressed in Japanese. In some cases, a word which automatically indicates plurality (such as **taku-san,** *many, much*—or a numeral) will convey the notion; sometimes the context will determine whether singular or plural is meant.

3. The few cases in which a plural suffix appears occur in nouns which refer to animate beings, usually human beings: **kodomo,** *child,* vs. **kodomo-ra** or **kodomo-tachi,** *children;* **sensei,** *teacher, doctor,* vs. **sensei-tachi** or **sensei-gata,** *teachers.* The form **gata** is more polite than **tachi** but the latter is used more. In some cases, this idea of plurality (or more accurately: of a group) is expressed by means of reduplication: **hito,** *man, human being,* vs. **hito-bito,** *people,* (for more examples and for the rules of the alternation involved, see p. 10 of Key to Pronunciation).

4. When in doubt about the use of a plural-suffix, it is best to leave it unused and to expand the context.

5. To indicate its relation to other nouns in the sentence or to the sentence as a whole, the noun may be followed by a limited number of particles which bear the entire burden of Japanese sentence formation.

PARTICLES

6. Generally speaking, particles never begin a sentence. For the most part, they can occur both after nouns and after verbs or adjectives.

7. The object of a verb precedes the verb and is indicated by means of the particle **o** as in **hon o yomimashita,** *I read a book;* **eiga o mimashita,** *I saw a movie.*

8. The particle **no** indicates that the noun which precedes it is the possessor and the noun which follows it the possessed: **Tōkyō no basu,** *Tokyo's buses;* **watakushi no chichi no uchi,** *my father's house;* **uchi no mado,** *the window of the house, the house's window.*

9. The particle **wa** can be translated as: *as concerns, as for,* and indicates a remote subject: **mado wa ōkii (desu),** *the window is big;* literally: *as concerns the window, it is big* (or: *there is bigness*). Other examples: **otōsan wa gohan o tabemashita,** *father ate the food;* **kono hon wa takakatta,** *this book was expensive;* **are wa samban desu,** *that is the number three (bus, train).*

10. To indicate a question, we attach the particle **ka** to the end of the sentence: **are wa samban desu ka?** *is that number three?* (literally: *as concerns that, is it a No. 3*). Other examples: **watakushi ka?** *I?;* **gohan ka,** *(are you talking about) food?;* **kono hon wa takakatta ka?** *was this book expensive?; was this an expensive book?.* Note that the particle **ka** may be called a verbal or spoken question mark.

11. If in the sentence (see 9) **otōsan wa gohan o tabemashita ka,** *did father eat the food (rice); has father had dinner?* we substitute **ga** for **wa,** the meaning changes to: *was it father who ate the rice?.* The particle **ga** thus expresses not a remote but an immediate subject. This distinction between "remote" and "immediate" may help the student to remember the important difference between **wa** and **ga.** The particles **wa** and **ga** can also occur in one and the same sentence: **otōsan wa mikan ga suki desu,** *father likes tangerines;* literally: *as concerns father, there is* (immediate) *liking of tangerines.* Also: **watakushi wa gaikokujin desu,** *I am a foreigner,* vs. **watakushi ga gaikokujin desu,** *I am the foreigner* (about whom something has already been said). See Personal Pronouns, p. 105.—Purists insist that the object of a

verb in the volitive (with **-tai**) must be indicated by **ga** and not, as in the case of all other objects, by **o**. Thus: **mizu ga nomitai,** (I) *want to drink water,* rather than **mizu o nomi-tai.** The latter form (with **o**) has been gaining more and more acceptance in recent years.

12.   The particle **e** indicates motion toward a place, direction, e. g., **Amerika e ikimashita,** (he) *went to America;* **uchi e kaette kimashita,** (he) *came returning home, he returned home;* **migi e magarimashita,** (I) *turned to the right;* **itsu minato e tsukimasu ka?** *when do (we) arrive in (to) the harbor?.*

13.   A more exact indication of direction, the point up to which the motion proceeds, is rendered by the particle **made;** e.g.: **Amerika made ikimashita,** (he) *went as far* (up to but no further than) *as America;* **mizu wa koko made hairimashita,** (the) *water came up to here* (up to this point). This particle can also be translated by *until* when we are concerned with time and by *even* when we are concerned with knowing, e.g.: **san-ji made uchi ni orimasu,** *I shall be home* (in the house) *until three o'clock;* **Sui-yōbi made,** *until Wednesday;* **inu no namae made shitte imasu,** *he knows it* (e.g., the family) *even to the name of the dog; he even knows the name of the dog.*

14.   When it follows a noun, the particle **kara** means *from,* e.g., **Tōkyō kara Amerika e ikimashita,** (he) *went from Tokyo to America;* **mado kara to made jū mētoru desu,** *it is ten metres from the window to the door;* **koko kara,** *from here* (on). Used with verbs or adjectives, **kara** may mean *because:* **furui kara yasui desu,** *it is cheap because it is old;* **Amerika e ikimashita kara,** *because he went to America;* **takusan taberu kara futotte imasu,** *he is fat because he eats a great deal.* With the converb (see p. 103), **kara** means *after,* e.g., **tabete kara eiga e ikimashō,** *let us go to the movies after we have eaten;* **kaette kara aimashita,** *I met him after I returned.* Summary: **kara** may mean *from, because,* or *after.*

15.   *Also* is rendered by the particle **mo,** e.g., **otōsan mo,**

father, too; **saru mo ki kara ochiru,** (proverb) *even a monkey may fall down from a tree,* i.e., *even an expert may slip;* **anata mo watakushi mo,** *you too, I too,* i.e., *both you and* I. **tabako mo yasui,** *cigarettes* (tobacco) *are also cheap.* As in the case of the proverb quoted here, **mo** may also mean *even* or *even if* after converbs: **tabako wa yasukute mo,** *even if tobacco is cheap;* **kaette mo...,** *even if I return*(see p. 103).

16.   General indication in space or time is indicated by **ni** as in **Amerika ni,** *in America;* **Sui-yōbi ni,** *on Wednesday,* when these are followed by verbs not containing the notion of movement. This same particle is also used to render Class II adjectives into adverbs, e.g., **shiawase ni,** *fortunately;* **fushiawase ni,** *unfortunately.* The function of **ni** as a space-and-time indicator is closely related to its function as an indicator of purpose: **mikan o kai ni ikimashita,** *he went* (out) *to buy tangerines;* **kodomo o sagashi ni ikimashita,** *she went to look for the child.* With verbs of giving and saying, we render **ni** by means of English *to:* **otōsan ni iimashita,** *he said* (it) *to father;* **watakushi ni kikimashita,** *he asked me* (*"to" me*). Summary: **ni** is translatable by means of: *on, in, (at,) in order to, -ly, to.*

17.   Location, when connected with a verb of action, is rendered by the particle **de** which also means *with, by means of;* e.g., **yama de kari o shimashita,** *they went hunting in the woods;* **fune de ikimashita,** *they went by boat;* **hasami de,** *with (a pair of) scissors;* **byoki de nete imasu,** *he is sick in bed,* i.e., *he is confined to bed with illness;* **doko de?** *where?, where at?* (plus action); **hitori de,** *alone; by oneself.*

18.   Addition in the sense of *and* is rendered by means of **to** as in **okāsan to otōsan,** *mother and father;* **uchi to niwa,** *house and garden.* This particle also stands for our closing quotation marks, e.g., **ara to iimashita,** *she said:"Well!...".* It is therefore also used in indirect quotations: **kaeru to iimashita,** *he said he would return* (i.e., he said **kaeru**); **mikan wa yasui to kikimashita,** *I heard that tangerines were (are) cheap.*

19. While the above grammatical particles all play essential roles in the structure of a sentence, another particle which normally appears in sentence-final position is **ne** (or **nē**). It indicates that the speaker is soliciting the hearer's approval, much like our expressions *well, you see* or *see what I mean?*, e.g., **mikan wa takai nē,** *tangerines are expensive, aren't they?*; **gaikokujin desu ne,** *well, you see, he (she) is a foreigner (and I...).* This particle is also used as a *filler* in awkward speech, as in: **watakushi wa ne Tōkyō e ne ikitai ne,** *well, er, I, er, want to, er, go to Tokyo.*

20. The grammatical particles discussed above can also be *heaped* upon one another, that is, they can appear in series usually of two, for example, **de mo** in **mikan de mo kekkō desu,** *(it does not matter) a tangerine will also do.* This sequence, **de mo,** may also begin a sentence: **De mo, ii hito desu,** *still, he is a good person.* **De mo** is also used to mean *even*: **kodoma de mo shitte imasu,** *even a child knows that.* The particle **mo** is particularly flexible in such combinations: **uchi ni mo,** *also in the house*; **hasami de mo,** *also with scissors*; **otōsan kara mo,** *also from father*; **doko made mo,** *anywhere*, i.e., *as far as anywhere*; **doko kara mo,** *from anywhere.* Causality can be expressed by **no de** as in: **byōki na no de,** *because he is ill*; *although* by **no ni**: **byōki de ita no ni,** *although he was ill.*

21. Note also: **no tame** or **no tame ni,** *for (something, someone)*: **kore o sensei no tame ni kaimashita,** *I bought this for the doctor*; **dake,** *only*: **mikan dake,** *only tangerines*; **zutsu,** *so many per unit,...each*: **sā futatsu zutsu,** *here you are, two apiece*; **yo,** *indeed*: **iku yo,** *but he is going, really*; **futatsu zutsu moraimashita yo,** *indeed, we received two apiece.*

THE ADJECTIVE

22. The Japanese adjective may carry the full weight of a verb; it may constitute the predicate of a sentence: **mikan wa yasui,** *tangerines are cheap.* But it may also have exactly the same function as it has in English, namely, to modify a following noun: **yasui mikan,** *cheap tangerines.*

23. An adjective such as **yasui** also resembles the Japanese verb in another respect: it can have tense-differences. The past of **yasui,** *cheap,* is **yasukatta.** Similarly:

akai	red	vs.	**akakatta**	was red
wakai	young		**wakakatta**	was young
atarashii	new		**atarashikatta**	was new
tsuyoi	strong		**tsuyokatta**	was strong
nurui	lukewarm		**nurukatta**	was lukewarm.

Rule: To form the past of an adjective which ends in **i** in the present, remove this **i** and substitute **-katta** in its place.

24. Let us class all those adjectives which end in **-i** in the present and in **-katta** in the past in Class I. These adjectives also have the following particularities, all reminiscent of the verbal system: (1) when an adjective of this class modifies a following verb (i. e., when it becomes an adverb), it loses its final **-i** and is then replaced by **-ku,** e.g., **nuruku nari mashita,** *it became lukewarm;* **tsuyoku miemashita,** *he looked strong.* (2) The conditional of such an adjective can be formed by substituting **-kereba** or **-kattara** for the final **-i** of the present: **akakereba** or **akakattara,** *if it were (is) red;* **wakake reba** or **wakakattara,** *if I were young.* (3) The negated form of such adjectives is obtained by removing the final **-i** of the present and attaching **-kunai** in its place: **tsuyokunai,** *(he is) not strong;* **akakunai,** *not red;* **atarashikunai,** *not new.* (4) The negated form can be again expanded in the manner of the adjective itself:

akakunai not red
akakunaku (narimashita) (he became) not red
akakunakatta was not red
akakunakereba
akakunakattara } would not be red

25. Another type of adjective which we shall call Class II lacks all of these inflections, e.g., **benri,** *useful,* literally, *usefulness* (a noun). When used to modify a noun, a Class II adjective must be enlarged by the suffix **-na: benri-na hasami,** *useful scissors;* **kirei-na niwa,** *a beautiful garden.* When used as an adverb (analogously to the **-ku** form of Class I adjectives), these adjectives are followed by the particle **ni** as in **kirei ni narimashita**, *she became beautiful;* **jōzu ni narimashita**, *he became adept* (*at...*). All other forms of Class II adjectives are formed by compounding:

kirei de wa nai ⎫
kirei de wa arimasen ⎬ she is not beautiful

kirei de wa arimasen deshita she was not beautiful
kirei de wa arimasen deshitara if she were not beautiful

In other words, except when followed by **-na** and the particle **ni,** Class II adjectives exhibit the same behavior as nouns.

26. Comparative adjectives can be formed with **motto,** *more, -er;* and superlatives with **ichiban** (lit., *number one*) or **mottomo,** *most, -est. Very* is expressed by **taihen, nakanaka** or **totemo.**

motto yasui cheaper
ichiban yasui the cheapest
taihen yasui ⎫
nakanaka yasui ⎬ very cheap
totemo yasui ⎭

27. Comparisons which require the use of *than* in English do not require a special form of the adjective in Japanese: **ringo wa mikan yori yasui,** *apples are cheaper than tangerines;* literally, *as concerns apples, tangerines-than are cheap.* Rule: the losing partner of the comparison is followed by **yori,** *than,* in Japanese., e.g., **anata wa watakushi yori wakai,** *you are younger than I.*

28. Note: the adjective **ii,** *good,* also has a slightly more formal variant: **yoi.** The latter is the form on which all the inflected forms are based:

yoi or **ii** good
yokatta was good
yoku well
yokunai not good
yokunakatta was not good
yokunakereba ⎫
yokunakattara ⎬ if it is not (were not) good

CARDINAL NUMBERS

29. There are two differently formed sets of Japanese numbers, which we can call Set I and Set II, depending on the noun to which the number refers. The two sets merge after 10, with a few exceptions. The general set (Set I) refers to unspecified things:

hitotsu	one	**muttsu**	six
futatsu	two	**nanatsu**	seven
mittsu	three	**yattsu**	eight
yottsu	four	**kokonotsu**	nine
itsutsu	five	**tō**	ten

Thus, **heya wa hitotsu,** *one room,* is literally "as concerns room(s), one". But the roots of this series of numerals can also combine with such words as **heya,** *room,* and yield combinations such as **hito-heya,** *one room;* **futa-heya,** *two rooms,* etc. Likewise, **hito-ban,** *one evening* (or *night*); **mi-ban,** *three nights,* etc. The questioning word which runs parallel to this series is **ikutsu,** *how many?* and its root can likewise combine with nouns, e.g., **iku-heya,** *how many rooms?*

30. The numbers of Set II run as follows:

ichi	one
ni	two
san	three
shi	four (also: **yon** or **yo,** as in **yo-ji** *4 o'clock*)
go	five
roku	six
shichi	seven
hachi	eight
kyū	nine (also: **ku**)
jū	ten

jū-ichi	11	**ni-jū**	20
jū-ni	12	**san-jū**	30
jū-san	13	**shi-jū** } **yon-jū**}	40
jū-shi } **jū-yon** }	14		
		go-jū	50
jū-go	15	**roku-jū**	60
jū-roku	16	**shichi-jū**	70
jū-shichi	17	**hachi-jū**	80
jū-hachi	18	**kyū-jū**	90
jū-kyū} **jū-ku** }	19	**hyakū**	100

ni-hyaku	200		ni-sen	2000
sam-byaku	300		san-zen	3000
yon-hyaku	400		yon-sen	4000
go-hyaku	500		gosen	5000
rop-pyaku	600		roku-sen	6000
nana-hyaku	700		nana-sen	7000
hap-pyaku	800		has-sen	8000
kyū-hyaku	900		kyū-sen	9000
sen	1000		man ⎫ ichi-man⎬	10,000
			sam-man	30,000 etc.

100,000 is **jū-man,** i.e., $10 \times 10,000$; 1,000,000 is **hyaku-man,** i.e., $100 \times 10,000$.

31. It is the second set of numbers, therefore, which continues after 10. It is used in the most common and useful expressions such as:

ichi ji	one o'clock	**san ji yon-jup-pun**	3:40 (a.m. or p.m.)
ichi jikan	one hour	**roku jikan han**	six and a half hours
ichi nen	one year	**jū nen**	ten years
ichi en	one yen	**hyaku san-jū-go en**	135 Yen
ichi do	once	**san do me**	the third time

THE VERB

32. To predicate something of something else, the Japanese language uses the copula **desu** in the present, **desita** in the past, **deshō** in cases of uncertainty and in the future, and **deshitara** in the conditional:

sore wa niwa desu that is a garden

sore wa niwa deshita that was a garden

sore wa niwa deshō that may be the garden; I think that that is the garden

sore wa niwa deshitara if that is a garden; if that were a garden

33. The negated form of the copula is: **de wa arimasen** (less polite, **de wa nai;** informal, **ja nai**), e.g.:

sore wa niwa de wa arimasen ⎫
sore wa niwa ja nai ⎬ that is not a garden; that's no garden

34. Thus the copula generally equates one thing with another. In addition, there are two other verbs in Japanese which are also translatable by *is* in English. The first, **arimasu,** means *there is* in general: **mikan ga arimasu,** *there* *is a tangerine; there are tangerines* (on hand). The second, **imasu,** means *lives, resides, is* when said of persons: **otōsan wa Tōkyō ni imasu,** *father is in Tokyo.* This verb also has another function, which will be discussed below.

35. It is important to note at this point that the Japanese verb does not distinguish, in its forms, between the third person and the other persons, as English does (he eats vs. I eat, you eat, we eat, they eat). One single form serves for all persons. On the other hand, the social context of a conversation is expressed in the language by the presence or absence of the "politeness-suffix".

A	B	ANY PERSON
taberu	**tabemasu**	eats
miru	**mimasu**	sees
neru	**nemasu**	sleeps
aruku	**arukimasu**	walks
kau	**kaimasu**	buys
kiku	**kikimasu**	hears, asks
iku	**ikimasu**	goes

Thus, the forms in columns A and B are similar, but the forms in column B tend to be favored in ordinary conversation among people who are not united by any particular social bond (family, school, army, club, profession). Broadly speaking, the forms in column A are used by interlocutors who have reason to feel that they belong to a closely-knit homogeneous group, e.g., classmates, soldiers of the same rank, brothers. It may also occur that one interlocutor uses forms from column A to another who replies with forms from column B. In this case, the speaker who uses A has confident reasons for doing so: age, social status, arrogance, urgency. We shall call the forms in column A "neutral" and the forms in column B "polite". Since foreigners speaking Japanese are not likely to be well-established members of an in-group, they are advised to use the polite forms.

36. Needless to say, every Japanese verb has a set of polite and a set of neutral forms. The neutral set is larger, for there are some grammatical categories which have no polite equivalents. The most important grammatical categories in the

verb are: the present which indicates an event whose place-
ment in time is vague or completely unspecified; the past; the
"future" which, in fact, expresses uncertainty or the unwilling-
ness on the part of the speaker to assume full responsibility
for his statement (this "future" is also a polite way of saying
let us); the conditional which expresses *if*-clauses; the negative; the volitive which expresses desire or need. There is also
an imperative (see p. 103), but its use is extremely restricted and
it should not be used by a foreigner. The model verb
for the following table is **taberu,** *to eat;* stem: **tabe-.**

NEUTRAL	SUFFIXES	POLITE	SUFFIXES	CATEGORY
taberu	-ru	tabemasu	-masu	Present
tabeta	-ta	tabemashita	-mashita	Past
tabeyō	-yō	tabemashō	-mashō	Future
tabereba	-reba	—		Conditional
tabenai	-nai	tabemasen	-masen	Negative
tabetai	-tai	—		Volitive

Suffixes are the inflected endings which are attached to the
stem when it appears in one or the other category. The
student should memorize them, for they are the key to
the entire Japanese verbal system. Verbs taking these
suffixes belong to the First Conjugation, which includes
such common verbs as **miru,** *see,* **neru,** *sleep,* **deru,** *go out,
exit, issue from,* **ochiru,** *fall.*

37. Inflection of verbs belonging to the Second Conjugation is essentially the same. The only differences which occur
are in phonetic modifications of the stems. Just as verbs
of the First Conjugation can be said to have vowel stems
(**tabe-**), so—broadly speaking—those of the Second can be
called consonantal-stem verbs, e.g.: **kiku,** *hear.*

NEUTRAL		POLITE		CATEGORY
kiku	-u	kikimasu	-imasu	Present
kiita	-ta	kikimashita	-imashita	Past
kikō	-ō	kikimashō	-imashō	Future
kikeba	-eba	—		Conditional
kikanai	-anai	kikimasen	-imasen	Negative
kikitai	-itai	—		Volitive

So also: **aruku, aruita, arukō, arukeba, arukanai, arukitai;**

arukimasu, arukimashita, arukimashō, arukimasen, *walk.*
Note that the stem remains the same throughout except for
the PAST. In the polite, the endings are the same as those of
the First Conjugation, except that they are preceded by an **i**
which remains constant throughout.

38. The stem in the case of the verb *hear* is **kik-**. In the
case of the verb *read* it is **yom-**. Again, the only departure
from this constant stem is in the past. The forms are: **yomu,
yonda, yomō, yomeba, yomanai, yomitai; yomimasu, yomimashita, yomimashō, yomimasen,** likewise in the case
of **yobu,** *to call* (stem: **yob-**): **yobu, yonda** (!), **yobō, yobeba,
yobanai; yobimasu,** etc.

39. In the case of the verb **omou,** *think* (and in all verbs
which end in **ou**), a **w** is inserted before the negative form
and, again, the past shows its irregularity: **omou, omotta,
omō, omoeba, omowanai, omoitai; omoimasu,** etc,

40. Other verbs of this conjugation (try to analyze the forms)
naru (*become*), **natta, narō, nareba, naranai, naritai; narimasu,** etc., **hanasu** (*tell* a story), **hanashita** (!), **hanasō, hana-
seba, hanasanai, hanashitai; hanashimasu,** etc., **motsu**
(*hold, have*), **motta, motō, moteba, motanai, mochitai** (!);
mochimasu, etc., (**t** changes to **ch** before **i**). **nuu** (*sew, stitch*),
nutta, nuō, nueba, nuwanai, nuitai; nuimasu, etc.

41. There are only two verbs which strongly diverge from
this pattern. They are **kuru,** *come,* and **suru,** *do, make:*

kuru	suru	Present
kita	shita	Past
koyo	shiyo	Future
kureba	sureba	Conditional
konai	shinai	Negative
kitai	shitai	Volitive
kimasu	shimasu	Polite: Present

42. The negative is the form from which further forms can
be derived:

Negative Present	tabenai	kikanai	konai	shinai
Past	tabenakatta	kikanakatta	konakatta	shinakatta
Conditional	tabenakereba	kikanakereba	konakereba	shinakereba
	eat	hear	come	do

These forms mean *does, did, would not eat*, etc.

43.   Further forms can be derived by attaching the so-called passive and causative elements: **taberareru, taberareta, taberaremashita,** *can be eaten, is eaten,* and **tabesaseru, tabesaseta, tabesasemashita,** *cause to eat, give to eat.* Such derived forms, when they do come up, had better be learned as new verbs.

44.   In discussing the categories of the verb we have purposely omitted one category which is of extreme importance. This is the CONVERB. It is formed exactly as the neutral past, with the only exception that where the neutral past has the vowel **a** (**tabeta, mita, kiita, yonda, kita**), the converb has the vowel **e**:

tabete	eating
mite	seeing
yonde	calling, reading (respectively from **yobu** and **yomu**)
kite	coming
aruite	walking
natte	becoming
nutte	stitching
hanashite	telling

The function of the converb is to form the progressive which corresponds to the English *is....-ing.* In the progressive the converb is followed by a form of the verb **imasu,** *is, resides,* etc. (see pp. 99–100):

tabete imasu	he is eating
yonde imashita	he was reading
nutte imasu	she is sewing

The converb is further used to modify another verb, much as in English: **aruite kimashita** *he came walking, he came a-walking* (that is, not by a conveyance).

45.   The polite imperative, by nature a request, is formed by adding **kudasai** (literally: *please condescend to*) to the converb:

yonde kudasai	please call (him), please read (it)
nutte kudasai	please sew (it)
tabete kudasai	please eat; help yourself

46.   Purpose clauses expressing the notion of *in order to* are formed by means of the infinitive of the verb followed by the particle **ni.** The infinitive of First Conjugation verbs (see **36**) is their mere stem: **tabe ni ikimashita,** *he went to eat,* **mi ni kimashita,** *he came to see.* The infinitive of Second Conjugation verbs (see p. 101) is easily obtained by removing **-masu** from **-imasu** with which the Polite-Present is formed thus: **arukimasu,** *he walks,* (infinitive: **aruki**), e.g., **yomi ni ikimashita,** *he went (somewhere) to read;* **nui ni kimashita,** *she came (here) to do some sewing.* The use of the infinitive is also important in stylistic-polite speech.

47. *The act of ...-ing* is expressed by the Neutral-Present (see pp. 100-101) plus **koto: aruku koto,** *walking, the act of walking;* **nuu koto wa dekimasen** *I can not sew* (**dekiru,** *to be able,* First Conj.); **yomu koto wa suki desu,** *I like to read.* The past infinitive is formed in the same way, using the Past as the point of departure. Its use is especially frequent in phrases of the type *I have never...,* e.g., **mita koto wa arimasen,** *I have never seen (it),* literally: *as concerns the act of having seen it, there (just) is not;* **tabeta koto wa arimasen,** *I have never eaten (it).*

48. A verb in the neutral (see pp. 100-101) past form may also modify a noun, e.g., **mita hon,** *the book which I have seen;* **tabeta mikan,** *the tangerine which has been eaten (which someone has eaten).*

DEMONSTRATIVE AND INTERROGATIVE PRONOUNS AND ADVERBS

49. There are three demonstrative pronouns, meaning *this* (near the speaker), *that* (not far from the speaker) and *that over yonder* (far from the speaker).

NEAR	NOT FAR	FAR	QUESTION
kore this thing	**sore** that thing	**are** yon thing	**dore** which thing?
kono this	**sono** that	**ano** yon	**dono** which?
konna such a	**sonna** such a	**anna** such a	**donna** what kind of a?
kō this way	**sō** so	**ā** that kind	**dō** how?
koko here	**soko** there	**asoko** yonder	**doko** where?
kochira here	**sochira** there	**achira** yonder	**dochira** where?

Examples: **kore wa niwa desu,** *this is a garden* (**kore** used

as a noun); **kono niwa wa furui desu,** *this garden is old;*
konna niwa wa kirei desu *such a garden is beautiful;* **kō
site kudasai,** *do* (*it*) *this way please;* **koko wa niwa desu,**
the garden is here; here is the garden; **kochira wa niwa desu,**
the garden is this way; **donna hito,** *what kind of a man?;*
doko no hito, *a man from where?;* **dō iu fū ni,** *in what way?;*
sō iu fū ni, *in such a way;* **dore,** *which* (*of a number of
things*)?

50. Note also: **donata,** *who?* (less polite: **dare,** *who?*).

51. Other question-words: **ikura,** *how much?,* **ikutsu,**
how many?, **iku-nin,** *how many persons?.* The very frequent
word **nani,** *what?* occurs as **nan** when it is compounded with
other words, e.g., **nan-ji,** *at what time,* literally: *what hour?;*
nan-nin, *how many persons?* (more common than **iku-nin**);
nan-desu ka, *what is it?,* **nan to iu,** *...called what?.*

PERSONAL PRONOUNS

52. Japanese does not have a pronominal system such as
the English I, you (thou), he, she, it; we, you (ye), they. There
are, to be sure, some nouns that take the place of these pronouns, namely:

watakushi I	**watakushi-tachi, ware-ra** we
anata you	**anata-tachi** you, you-all
ano kata that person	
ano hito that man	
kare he	
kanojo she	

The student should remember that the use of any of these,
except **watakushi,** may involve a slight breach of etiquette
(in Japanese: **shitsurei**) which, though readily excused by the
Japanese, may result in an uncomfortable situation.   Thus
it is safest to avoid all translations of English pronouns, and
to use titles and names as much as possible.

53. If a Japanese has a title, it is safe to address him by it.
Also teachers at all levels and physicians are addressed by
the title **sensei** (literally, *first-born, elder*).   In other cases, a

person's profession, followed by **-san,** *Mr., Mrs., Miss,* will do equally well. Thus a taxi-driver or a bus-driver can be addressed by the title **untenshu-san,** *Mr. Chauffeur,* which will serve much better than **anata.** Similarly, **yūbinya-san wa Tōkyō no kata desu ka,** *is Mr. Post (Mail) a person from Tokyo, i.e., are you from Tokyo, Mr. Mailman?* is in much better style than **anata wa...**

54. The term **watakushi** may be more readily used, but one may indicate humility by referring to oneself as **kochira** (literally, *in this direction*).

55. A festive variant of **-san** is **-sama,** which is used especially with God, in **Kami-sama.**

56. Kinship terminology is important to the beginner insofar as he should remember that *my father* is **chichi** and *my mother,* **haha,** whereas *your father* or *his father* are **otōsan** or **otōsama** and *your mother* or *his mother,* **okāsan.** A very important exception, however, is that within the home, the children address their father and mother as **otōsan** and **okāsan.** Thus, **chichi** and **haha** are only used when speaking to outsiders about one's own parents.

57. Similarly: **onii-san,** *your elder brother* or *his elder brother;* **ani,** *my elder brother;* **ōnē-san,** *your elder sister;* **ane,** *my elder sister.*

SYNTAX

58. The three basic elements of the Japanese sentence which must occupy a specific position in the sequence of speech are the subject (particle **ga**), the object (particle **o**), and the predicate (verb). The rule governing the position of the predicate as the last element of the sentence always holds.

Subject + ga + object + o + verb.

59. As a rule, the subject precedes the object, but in cases of strong emphasis, the order may at times be reversed, e. g., **sore o sensei ga kakimashita,** *that one was written by tea-*

cher; compare the normal order: **sensei ga sore o kakima-shita,** *teacher wrote that one;* literally, *teacher* (subject), *that one* (object), *wrote.*

> **Object + o + subject + ga + verb.**

60. The remote subject (particle **wa**) usually stands at the beginning of the sentence, but its position there is not as firm as, say, that of the subject. In fact, the remote subject's position is very loose and very often, when the context is clear, the Japanese will omit it all together. This happens especially when one introduces oneself. The formula is: **watakushi wa Tana-ka desu,** *my name is Tanaka;* literally, *as concerns me, it is Tanaka.* But, on most informal occasions, the speaker will content himself with: **Tanaka desu,** *(it is) Tanaka.*

> **Remote subject + wa + immediate subject + ga + verb.**

FORMAL LANGUAGE

61. We have seen that the verb can be neutral or polite, e.g., **taberu** vs. **tabemasu** (See pp. 100-101). Besides this device, there are several other ways of expressing formality.

62. One of these is to prefix **o-** and **go-** to certain nouns or adjectives, usually to show respect toward the possessor or merely to convey the thought that the subject of discussion is his possession: **hon,** *book* vs. **go-hon,** *your book;* **uchi,** *house* vs. **o-uchi,** *your house;* **tanjōbi,** *birthday* vs. **o-tanjōbi,** *your birthday;* **takai,** *expensive* vs. **o-takai,** *expensive* (said with intimidation or respect); **kuni,** *country* vs. **o-kuni,** *your country;* **kotoba,** *words, speech* vs. **o-kotoba,** *your words.*

63. Another device for expressing formality is through employing intrinsically exalted words, e.g., **meshiagaru,** *to eat;* **mesu,** *to wear;* **irassharu,** *to come, go;* **itsu irasshaima-su ka,** *when are you coming (to visit us)?*

64. The infinitive preceded by **o-** and followed by the particle **ni** and forms of the verb **narimasu,** *to become,* is also employed in this way: **o-kai ni narimashita ka,***did you buy* (*it*)? (from **kau,** *buy*); **o-yomi ni narimasen ka,** *won't you read it?* (i.e., *please do*). Similar to this construction is **go-ran ni naru,** *to see, look:* **go-ran ni narimashita ka,** *have you seen it;* **go-ran ni naremasu,** *you can see it.*

65. There are also a few humble words which reverse the process, indicating that the speaker places himself in a humble position: **haiken itashimasu,** *I* (*shall*) *take a look at it;* (where **itashimasu** is a humble form of **shimasu,** and **haiken** stands for *a viewing of it*).

66. Such forms border on the literary language and the beginner need not make an effort to familiarize himself with them until a later stage of his studies.

STYLISTIC HINTS

67. Avoid the use of a translation of English 'must' or 'have to'. We abuse this verb in such expressions as 'I have to go and get some soap'; the Japanese resort to it only when they really mean that circumstances compel the speaker to do something. The expression then is: **sekken o kawanakereba narimasen,** literally: *If I do not buy soap* (*the whole thing*) *will come to nothing.* In such cases it is best to survey the situation and express it through other means, such as: **sekken wa mō naku narimashita,** *there is not more soap,* literally: *the soap has already disappeared* (or *come to its end*).

68. Avoid the use of 'can' in such contexts as 'Can you tell me where...', 'Can I trouble you for...'. The verb *to be able* is **dekiru** (see p. 104), but its basic meaning is, in fact, *to get something done, to manage to, to finish something,* e.g., **sentaku wa dekimashita ka,** *is the laundry ready?* The polite way of asking for help, a favor, and the like is to present the request in the negative interrogative: *won't you, don't you?* e.g., **o-cha o ippai kudasaimasen ka,** *won't you give me a cup of tea?* (**ippai,** *one cup*); **ano kata no namae o oshiete kudasaimasen ka,** *can you tell me what his name is,* i.e., *won't you teach me* (with condescension) *that person's name?*

JAPANESE-ENGLISH DICTIONARY

The two-way dictionary of almost 5000 entries includes all the vocabulary used in the *Everyday Conversations* as well as many other high-frequency words and phrases used in everyday speech. Parts of speech are given when necessary; and each entry appears in its English, Japanese and transliterated forms.

A

abekobe *n.* あべこべ
the reverse, upside down, the contrary

abekobe no *adj.* あべこべの
reverse, contrary, upside down

abunai *adj.* 危ない dangerous

abura *n.* 油 oil, fat, grease

achira *adv.* あちら there

agaru *vi.* 上がる 1. go up, rise 2. eat, take, drink (when referred to food & beverage)
agarimasu (polite) 上がります

ageru *vt.* 上げる 1. give, offer 2. raise, lift up
agemasu (polite) 上げます

ai 愛 *n.* **aijō** 愛情 love, affection
aisuru *vt.* 愛する to love
aishimasu (polite) 愛します

aida *n.* 間 between, while, during

aikyō *n.* 愛嬌 charm, attractiveness

aimai *n.* あいまい vagueness, ambiguity

aimai na *adj.* あいまいな vague, ambiguous

aisatsu *n.* 挨拶 greeting

aisukurimu *n.* アイスクリーム ice cream

aita *adj.* 空いた empty, vacant, unoccupied, unengaged

aji *n.* 味 taste, flavor

aka *n.* 赤,紅 red

akai *adj.* 赤い,紅い red

akambō *n.* 赤ん坊 baby

akarui *adj.* 明るい bright, light

akeru *vt.* 開ける open, unlock
akemasu (polite) 開けます

aki *n.* 秋 autumn

akirameru *vt.* 諦める give up, abandon
akiramemasu (polite) 諦めます

akiru *vi.* 飽きる be tired of
akimasu (polite) 飽きます

aku *vi.* 開く open, be opened
akimasu (polite) 開きます

akushu *n.* 握手 handshaking

amai *adj.* 甘い sweet

ame *n.* 雨 rain
ama-gu *n.* 雨具 rainwear
ama-gutsu *n.* 雨靴 rain shoes, galoshes

ana *n.* 穴 hole

anata *pron.* あなた you
anata-tachi あなたたち you (plural)

anata no あなたの your (yours)

ane *n.* 姉 elder sister
o-nē san (polite) お姉さん

anna *adj.* あんな like that, that sort of, such as

annaisuru *vt.* 案内する guide, show
annaishimasu (polite) 案内します

ano *adj.* あの that, those

anshin *n.* 安心 peace of mind

anshinsuru *vi.* 安心する feel easy, set one's mind at rest, feel relieved

anshinshimasu (polite) 安心します

anzen na adj. 安全な safe, sure, secure, reliable

ao n. 青 blue

aoi adj. 青い blue

ao-zora 青空 blue sky

appuru pai n. アップルパイ apple pie

arai adj. 荒い rude, violent, harsh, rough

arai adj. 粗い coarse

arashi n. 嵐 storm, tempest, typhoon

arau vt. 洗う wash

araimasu (polite) 洗います

are pron. あれ that

Arigatō (gozaimasu) 有難う (ございます) Thank you

arimasen vi. ありません there is no, we don't have

aru vi. ある be, there is (are), have, be situated

arimasu (polite) あります

aruku vi. 歩く walk

arukimasu (polite) 歩きます

asa n. 朝 morning

asa-han 朝飯 breakfast

Ohayō (gozaimasu) お早よう(ございます) Good morning

asatte n. 明後日 day after tomorrow

ashita n. 明日 tomorrow

asobu vi. 遊ぶ play, amuse (or enjoy) oneself

asobimasu (polite) 遊びます

asoko adv. あそこ over there, there

asu n. adv. 明日 tomorrow

asuko あすこ yonder

atama n. 頭 head

atarashii adj. 新しい new

atatakai adj. 暖かい warm, mild

atena n. 宛名 address

ato n. 後 the back

ato ni 後に **ato de** 後で adj. later, after

atsui adj. 暑い hot

atsui adj. 熱い very warm

atsui adj. 厚い thick

atsumaru vi. 集まる come together

atsumarimasu (polite) 集まります

atsumeru vt. 集める gather, collect

atsumemasu (polite) 集めます

au vt. 合う fit, suit, be suited, harmonize, agree

aimasu (polite) 合います

au vt. 会う see, meet, interview

aimasu (polite) 会います

awai adj. 淡い light, faint

awaseru vt. 合わせる put together, unite, combine, connect

awasemasu (polite) 合わせます

ayashii adj. 怪しい doubtful, dubious, suspicious, questionable

azukaru vt. 預かる keep, take charge of, be entrusted with

azukarimasu (polite) 預かります

azukeru vt. 預ける entrust, deposit

azukemasu (polite) 預けます

B

baai n. 場合 case, occasion, time, circumstance

bai n. 倍 double, twice, twofold, two times

baka n. 馬鹿 fool, idiot

bakari adv. ばかり about, around

bakuzen n. 漠然 vagueness

bakuzen to *adv*. 漠然と vaguely, ambiguously, obscurely

bakuzen to shita *adj*. 漠然とした ambiguous

ban *n*. 番 number, one's turn

ban *n*. 晩 evening
   maiban *n*. 毎晩 every evening

banshu *n*. 晩秋 late autumn

banshun *n*. 晩春 late spring

bara *n*. ばら rose

basho *n*. 場所 1. place, spot, position, location, situation, scene, site 2. space, room 3. seat

basu *n*. バス bus

bata *n*. バター butter

Beikoku *n*. 米国 *or* **Amerika** アメリカ America (both are commonly used)

Beikoku-jin 米国人 American
Beikoku no *adj*. American

bēkon *n*. ベーコン bacon

bengoshi *n*. 弁護士 lawyer, attorney

benjo *n*. 便所 toilet, wash-room (most signs use **benjo**)
   Polite forms: **go-fujō** ご不浄
   o-tearai お手洗い

benkyō *n*. 勉強 study
   benkyō suru *vi, vt*, 勉強する
   benkyō shimasu (polite) 勉強
   します

benkyōka *n*. 勉強家 diligent person

benri *n*. 便利 convenience, handiness

benri na *adj*. 便利な convenient, handy

beru *n*. ベル bell

betsu no *adj*. 別の separate, different, another

bifuteki *n*. ビフテキ beefsteak

bijutsu *n*. 美術 art

bijutsu-kan *n*. 美術館 art gallery

bikkuri suru *vi*. びっくりする be surprised, be amazed, be alarmed, be astonished
   bikkuri shimasu (polite) びっ くりします

bimbō *n*. 貧乏 poverty, destitution

bimbō na *adj*. 貧乏な poor, hard-up, indigent

bin *n*. 瓶 bottle

biru *n*. ビール beer

biyōin *n*. 美容院 hairdresser

biyō-taiso 美容体操 calisthenics

bō *n*. 棒 bar, pole

bōeki *n*. 貿易 trade, commerce
   gaikoku bōeki 外国貿易 foreign trade
   Note: **bōeki** alone often refers to foreign trade

bōshi *n*. 帽子 hat, cap

botan *n*. ボタン button, stud, knob.
   botan o kakeru *vi*. ボタンを かける

botchan *n*. 坊ちゃん boy, son
   o-botchan お坊ちゃん your son (in conversation)

bu *n*. 部 part, portion

bubun *n*. 部分 part, portion

buji *n*. 無事 safety, security

buji na *adj*. 無事な safe, secure

bukkyō *n*. 仏教 Buddhism

bukkyō bijutsu 仏教美術 Buddhist art

bumpō *n*. 文法 grammar

bungaku *n*. 文学 literature
   kindai bungaku 近代文学 modern literature
   koten bungaku 古典文学 classic literature
   taishū bungaku 大衆文学 popular literature.

bunshi 文士 literary man, writer

bunka *n*. 文化 culture, civilization **bunka shisetsu** 文化施設 cultural institutions

bunka no kōryū 文化の交流 cultural exchange

burausu n. ブラウス blouse

burōchi n. ブローチ brooch

butai n. 舞台 stage

buyōjin na adj. 不用心な
1. insecure, unsafe, unreliable
2. imprudent, careless

byōin n. 病院 hospital

byōki n. 病気 sickness, illness, ailment, disease

byōnin n. 病人 sick person, a patient

C

cha n. 茶 tea **o-cha** (polite) お茶 **kō-cha** 紅茶 black tea **ryoku-ha** 緑茶 green tea **chado** 茶道 tea ceremony **cha-no-yu** 茶の湯 tea ceremony, tea cult **chawa-kai** 茶話会 (or **sawa-kai**) tea party

chairo n. 茶色 brown

chairo no adj. brown

chakkari shita adj. ちゃっかりした shrewd, cunning

chaku-chaku to adv. 着々と steadily, gets on smoothly

chanto adv. ちゃんと
1. in good order, properly
2. exactly, precisely

chawan n. 茶碗 rice bowl

chi n. 血 blood

chichi n. 父 father **o-tōsan** (polite) お父さん

chigau vi. 違う differ, vary **chigaimasu** (polite) 違います be dissimilar, be wrong

chigatta adj. 違った different, various, diverse

chihō n. 地方 area, region, district, locality

chiimu n. チーム team

chiisai adj. 小さい small, little, tiny or **chiisana** adj. 小さな

chiizu n. or **chizu** チーズ cheese

chijimeru vt. 縮める contract, shorten, shrink, dwindle **chijimemasu** (polite) 縮めます

chika n. 地下 basement, underground

chikatetsu 地下鉄 subway

chikagoro adv. 近頃 recently, lately, nowadays

chikagoro no adj. 近頃の recent

chikai adj. 近い 1. near, close 2. short, immediate

chika-michi n. 近道 short cut

chikara n. 力 strength, force

chikuji adv. 逐次 one by one, one after another, successively, in order

chikyū n. 地球 the earth, the globe

chippu n. チップ tip

chiri n. 地理 geography

chiri n. 塵 dust

chirigami n. 塵紙 toilet paper

chiryō n. 治療 medical treatment

chiryō suru vt. 治療する treat, cure

chishiki n. 知識 knowledge, learning

chizu n. 地図 map

chōba n. 帳場 counter, office (of a hotel)

chōchin n. 提燈 (paper) lantern

chōdai suru 頂戴する receive, accept, get, be presented with, take, eat, drink **chōdaishimasu** (polite) 頂戴します

chōdo adv. ちょうど just, exactly, precisely, right

chōkoku *n.* 彫刻 sculpture, carving

chōmiryō *n.* 調味料 seasoning

chōsa *n.* 調査 check, investigation, inquiry

chōsa suru *vt.* 調査する investigate

chōsetsu suru *vt.* 調節する regulate, adjust, control
  chōsetsushimasu (polite) 調節します

chotto *adv.* ちょっと just a little, just a minute

chūi *n.* 注意 1. attention, notice 2. care, precaution, caution 3. advice

chūi sure *vt.* 注意する 1. pay attention to; attend to 2. beware of, be cautious of 3. advise, give advice to 4. warn
  chūi shimasu polite(注意)します

chūmon *n.* 注文 an order

chūmon suru *vt.* 注文する place an order, request, ask
  chūmon shimasu (polite) 注文します

chūnen *n.* 中年 middle age
  chūnen no *adj.* 中年の middle-aged
  chūnen no shinshi 中年の紳士 middle-aged, gentleman

chūsha *n.* 注射 injection

chūsha (o) suru *vt.* 注射(を)する give an injection

chushin *n.* 中心 center, core

D

daburu *vi.* ダブる be doubled, be duplicated, be repeated

daibu *adv.* だいぶ very much, greatly, considerably, rather

daidokoro *n,* 台所 kitchen, cuisine

daigaku *n.* 大学 university, college

dai-ichi ni *adv.* 第一に in the first place, firstly, to begin with

daiji na *adj.* 大事な important, serious, precious

daijōbu *adj.* 大丈夫 1. safe, secure, all right 2. certainly, undoubtedly, surely

daitai ni *adv.* 大体に on the whole, in general

dakara *conj.* だから 1. so, so that, therefore, accordingly 2. because of, since

dake *adv.* だけ 1. only, but, alone 2. as much as, as far as, so far as

dakyō *n.* 妥協 compromise, mutual concession, understanding

dakyōsuru *vi.* 妥協する compromise, come to terms with, meet (a person) halfway
  dakyōshimasu (polite) 妥協します

damasu *vt.* だます cheat, deceive, fake

damasareru *vi.* だまされる be cheated, be deceived, be fooled
  damasaremasu (polite) だまされます

dame na *adj.* 駄目な not good, no use, futile, in vain, fruitless

dame ni suru 駄目にする spoil, ruin, waste, bring (a plan) to nothing
  dame ni shimasu (polite) 駄目にします

dandan to *adv.* だんだんと gradually, little by little, step by step

dantai *n.* 団体 organization, corporation, association

darashinai *adj.* だらしない untidy, slovenly, loose

dare *pron.* 誰 who

dāsu *n.* ダース dozen

deguchi *n.* 出口 an exit

dekakeru *vi.* 出かける go out, set (off)

　dekakemasu(polite)出かけます

dekiagari *n.* 出来上がり completion, finish

dekimasen *vi.* 出来ません cannot do

　dekiru *vi.* 出来る can, be able to, be done, be completed, be made

　dekimasu (polite) 出来ます

dekki *n.* デッキ deck

de mo でも 1. even 2. as well, also 3. though, even if 4. still, but yet

demokurashii *n.* デモクラシー (or **minshushugi**) 民主民義 democracy

demonsutorēshon *n.* デモンストレーション demonstration

dempō *n.* 電報 telegram

dengon *n.* 伝言 message

dengon suru *vt.* 伝言する give a message to

denki *n.* 電気 electricity

denki mōfu 電気毛布 electric blanket

denki no *adj.* 電気の electric

denkyū 電球 electric bulb

densha *n.* 電車 streetcar

dentō 電灯 electric light

dentō *n.* 伝統 tradition, convention

denwa 電話 *n.* telephone

denwa kōkanshu 電話交換手 telephone operator

depāto *n.* デパート department

(store)

deru *vi.* 出る appear, come out, emerge, go out, step out, start, leave, depart

　demasu (polite) 出ます

deshita *vi.* でした was, it was

deshō *vi.* でしょう I think, I suppose, I guess, I hope, I expect, probably, possibly, perhaps

desu *vi.* です is, it is, it is a case of

de wa *conj.* で は then, well, in that case, if so

dezāto *n.* デザート dessert

dō *adv.* どう how

doa *n.* ドアー door

dōbutsu *n.* 動物 animal

dōbutsu-en 動物園 zoo

dōbutsu-gaku 動物学 zoology

dochira *adv.* どちら which one, where

do itashimashite どう致しまして not at all, don't mention it

dōjō 同情 sympathy

dōjō suru 同情する sympathize

　dōjōshimasu(polite)同情します

doko *adv.* どこ where

dōmo *adv.* どうも very much, quite, really

donaru *vi.* どなる cry out, shout, bawl

donata *pron.* どなた who, any one, somebody

donna *adj.* どんな what, what sort of

dono *adj.* どの which, what

dono kurai *adv.* どのくらい how far, how long, how soon, how much, how many, how large, how deep, how wide, how heavy

dore *pron.* どれ which

dorobō *n.* 泥棒 thief, burglar, robber

doru *n.* ドル dollar

dōse *adv.* どうせ any way, any how, at any rate, in any case

dōshite *adv.* どうして why

dōshite mo *adv.* どうしても by all means, at all costs

dotchi *pron.* どっち which

dotchi no *adj.* which

Do-yōbi *n.* 土曜日 Saturday

dōzo *adv.* どうぞ please (entreating)

   dōzo yoroshiku どうぞよろ しく please give my regards to

E

e *n.* 絵 picture, painting, drawing

e *n.* 柄 handle, knob, shaft

ebicha *n.* えび茶 maroon, brownish

   ebicha (iro) no *adj.* えび茶 (色) の maroon

eiga *n.* 映画 movie, cinema, motion picture

Eigo *n.* 英語 English

Eikoku *n.* 英国 **Igirisu** *or* England イギリス (both are commonly used)

   Eikoku-jin 英国人 Englishman, Englishwoman

eikyō *n.* 影響 influence, effect

   eikyō suru *vt.* 影響する influence, affect

   eikyō shimasu (polite) 影響し ます

eki *n.* 駅 station

   ekiben 駅弁 station luncheon

empitsu *n.* 鉛筆 pencil

   empitsu-kezuri 鉛筆削 pencil sharpener

en *n.* 円 yen

en *n.* 円 circle

enerugii *n.* エネルギー energy

enki *n.* 延期 postponement, deferment

   enki suru *vt.* 延期する postpone, put off

   enki shimasu (polite) 延期し ます

enryo *n.* 遠慮 reserve

   enryo suru *vi.* 遠慮する be reserved, hesitate

   enryo shimasu (polite) 遠慮し ます

   enryo-bukai *adj.* 遠慮深い reserved, modest

   Go-enryo naku meshiagatte kudasai 御遠慮なく召し上っ てください please help yourself (to something to eat)

   Tabako wa go-enryo kudasai タバコは御遠慮下さい please refrain from smoking

erabu *vt.* 選ぶ choose, select, prefer

   erabimasu (polite) 選びます

erebētā *n.* エレベーター elevator

esukarētā *n.* エスカレーター escalator

F

fōku *n.* フォーク fork

fuan *n.* 不安 uneasiness, anxiety

   fuan na *adj.* 不安な uncertain, insecure

   fuan ni omou *vt.* 不安に思う feel ill at ease, feel uneasy

fuben *n.* 不便 inconvenience, unhandiness

   fuben na *adj.* 不便な inconvenient, unhandy

fuchi *n.* 縁 edge, brim, rim,

frame

fuchūi *n.* 不注意 carelessness, thoughtlessness, imprudence

fuchūi na *adj.* 不注意な careless, inattentive, heedless, imprudent

fuhei *n.* 不平 discontent, displeasure

fuhei o iu *vi.* 不平を言う complain, gripe

　fuhei o iimasu (polite) 不平を 言います

fui no *adj.* 不意の sudden, unexpected, abrupt

fuirumu *n.* フィルム film

　karā fuirumu カラーフィルム color film

fuji-iro *n.* 藤色 light purple, lilac, mauve

fujiiro no *adj.* light purple

fujin *n.* 婦人 lady, woman

fukai *adj.* 深い deep

fukasa *n.* 深さ depth

fukkō *n.* 復興 rehabilitation, reconstruction

fuku *vi.* 吹く blow

　fukimasu (polite) 吹きます

fuku *vt.* 拭く wipe, mop

　fokimasu (polite) 拭きます

fukuro *n.* 袋 bag, sack

　kaimono-bukuro 買物袋 shopping bag

fukusō *n.* 服装 dress, costume, attire, clothes

fukuzatsu na *adj.* 複雑な complicated, complex

fun 分 a minute

　ippun 一分 one minute

　ni-fun 二分 two minutes

　sanjuppun 三十分 thirty minutes

funa bin *n.* 船便 sea mail

funayoi *n.* 船酔い seasickness

fune *n.* 船 ship, boat

fun-iki *n.* 雰囲気 atmosphere

Furansu *n.* フランス France

　Furansujin *n.* フランス人 French **Furansu-go** *n.* フランス語 French (language)

　Furansu no *adj.* フランスの French

furasshi barubu *n.* フラッシバ ルブ flashbulb

furo *n.* 風呂 bath

　o-furo (polite) お風呂

　furo ni hairu *vi.* 風呂に入る take bath

furui 古い *adj.* old, ancient

furu *vi.* 降る fall, come down (rain, snow, hail)

　furimasu (polite) 降ります

　Ame ga furimasu 雨が降り ます It rains

　Yuki ga furi sōdesu 雪が降り そうです It looks like snow

furumau *vi.* 振舞う act, behave

　furumaimasu (polite) 振舞い ます

futatsu *n.* 二つ two

　futsuka 二日 two days, the second day

futō *n.* 封筒 envelope

futoi *adj.* 太い 1. big, thick 2. deep (voice), sonorous

futon *n.* ふとん quilt

futsū no *adj.* 普通の ordinary, regular, common, usual, normal, average

fuyu *n.* 冬 winter

G

gaijin *n.* 外人 foreigner

　gaikoku *n.* 外国 foreign country, abroad

　gaikokujin 外国人 foreigner

gake *n.* 崖 cliff

gakkō *n.* 学校 school
  gakusei 学生 student
  gakusha 学者 scholar
ganjō na *adj.* 頑丈な solid, strong, stout
ganko na *adj.* 頑固な stubborn, obstinate, bigoted, stiff-necked, headstrong, persistent
garasu *n.* ガラス glass
gasorin *n.* ガソリン gasoline
gasu *n.* ガス gas
geijutsu *n.* 芸術 art
  geijutsu-ka 芸術家 artist
geki *n.* 劇 play, drama
gekijō *n.* 劇場 theater
genki *n.* 元気 vigor, spirit
genki na *adj.* 元気な in good spirits, healthy
  genki no yoi *adj.* 元気のよい full of energy
genkin *n.* 現金 cash
genzō *n.* 現像 development (of a picture)
  genzo suru *vt.* 現像する develop (picture)
geta *n.* 下駄 wooden clogs
Getsu-yōbi *n.* 月曜日 Monday
gimon *n.* 疑問 question, doubt
  gimon o motsu *vt.* 疑問をもつ doubt
gimu *n.* 義務 duty, obligation
  gimu o tsukusu 義務を尽す performs one's duty
ginkō *n.* 銀行 bank
go- 御 *honorific prefix*
go *n.* 五 five
  gojū-go *n.* 五十五 fifty-five
  goji 五時 five o'clock
gochagocha no ごちゃごちゃの mixed-up, confused, pell-mell
gofujō *n.* ご不浄 toilet, washroom
Go-gatsu *n.* 五月 May

gogo *n.* 午後 p.m., afternoon
gohan *n.* 御飯 cooked rice, meal
gokai *n.* 誤解 misunderstanding
gokai suru *vt.* 誤解する misunderstand
  gokai shimasu (polite) 誤解します
gōkei *n.* 合計 total
goku *adv.* ごく very, exceedingly, extremely, most
gomakasareru *vi.* ごまかされる be cheated, be deceived
  gomakasaremasu (polite) ごまかされます
gomakasu *vt.* ごまかす cheat, deceive
  gomakashimasu (polite) ごまかします
Gomen kudasai 御免下さい Excuse me, Pardon me
goraku *n.* 娯楽 recreation, entertainment, amusement
goraku-shitsu 娯楽室 recreation room
gorufu *n.* ゴルフ golf
  gorufu kōsu ゴルフコース golf course
gozaimasen *vi.* ございません there is no, we don't have, (humble form of **arimasen**)
gozaimasu *vi.* ございます there is, we have (*humble form of* **arimasu**)
gozen *n.* 午前 a.m., morning
guai *n.* 具合 condition
  tenki guai 天気具合 condition of the weather
  karada guai 体具合 condition of health
gūzen *n.* 偶然 chance
  gūzen ni *adv.* 偶然に by chance, accidentally
  gūzen no *adj.* 偶然の accidental

gyaku no *adj.* 逆の opposite, reverse, contrary, inverse

gyōgi *n.* 行儀 manners, behavior

gyōsei *n.* 行政 administration

gyōseki *n.* 業績 achievements, results

gyūniku *n.* 牛肉 beef

gyūniku-ya 牛肉屋 butcher

H

ha *n.* 歯 tooth

ha isha 歯医者 dentist

haba *n.* 幅 width, breath

habuku *vt.* 省く 1. exclude, eliminate, leave out 2. reduce, save, curtail

habukimasu (polite) 省きます

hachi *n.* 八 eight

hachijū-hachi 八十八 eighty-eight

Hachi-gatsu *n.* 八月 August

hade na *adj.* 派手な gay, loud

hagaki *n.* 葉書 post card

e-hagaki 絵葉書 picture post card

haha *n.* 母 mother

okāsan (polite) お母さん

hai *adv.* はい yes

hai *n.* 灰 ash

haizara 灰皿 ashtray

hairu *vi.* 入る enter, come in

hairimasu (polite) 入ります

hajimaru *vi.* 始まる begin, start

hajimarimasu (polite) 始まります

hajimeru *vt.* 始める begin, start

hajimemasu (polite) 始めます

hajimete *adv.* 初めて for the first time

hakkiri to *adv.* はっきりと 1. clearly, plainly 2. definitely

hakobu *vt.* 運ぶ carry, convey, transport

hakobimasu (polite) 運びます

hakubutsukan *n.* 博物館 museum

hambun *n.* 半分 half

hamu *n.* ハム ham

han *n.* 半 half

hana *n.* 花 flower, blossom

hana-mi 花見 flower-viewing

hana *n.* 鼻 nose

hanaji 鼻血 nosebleed

hanasu *vi. vt.* 話す talk, speak

hanashimasu (polite) 話します

hankachi *n.* ハンカチ handkerchief

harau *vt.* 払う 1. pay, settle one's account 2. brush off, clear

haraimasu (polite) 払います

hari *n.* 針 needle

haru *n.* 春 spring

haruka ni *adv.* 遙かに far away, in the distance

hasami *n.* 鋏 scissors

hashi *n.* 箸 chopsticks

hashi *n.* 橋 bridge

hashi *n.* 端 edge, tip, end

hashiru *vi.* 走る run, dash

hashirimasu (polite) 走ります

hasu *n.* 蓮 lotus

hata *n.* 旗 flag, banner

hataraku *vi.* 働く work

hatarakimasu (polite) 働きます

hato *n.* 鳩 pigeon, dove

hayai *adj.* 早い early

hayaku *adv.* 早く early

hayai *adj.* 速い quick, fast, swift

hayaku *adv.* 速く quickly, fast, swiftly

hayame ni *adv.* 早目に a little early

hayari *n.* 流行 fashion, fad

hayaru *vi.* 流行る be in fashion, grow in popularity

  hayarimasu (polite) 流行ります

hei *n.* 塀 wall, fence

heibon *n.* 平凡 commonness, platitude

heibon na *adj.* 平凡な common, ordinary

heiwa *n.* 平和 peace

henji *n.* 返事 answer, reply

henji (o) suru *vt.* 返事(を)する answer, reply

hen na *adj.* 変な strange, odd, queer

heta na *adj.* 下手な poor, clumsy, unskillful, awkward

heya *n.* 部屋 room

hi *n.* 日 sun, day

hi *n.* 火 fire

  kaji 火事 fire, conflagration

hi *n.* 灯 light

hidari *n.* 左 left

hidari-gawa 左側 left side

hidoi *adj.* ひどい severe, hard, awful, dreadful, cruel

hifu *n.* 皮膚 skin

higashi *n.* 東 east

higeki *n.* 悲劇 tragedy

hihyō *n.* 批評 criticism, review, comment

hihyō suru *vt.* 批評する criticize

  hihyō shimasu (polite) 批評します

hijō ni *adv.* 非常に very much, extremely, greatly

hikinobashi *n.* 引伸し enlargement

hikinobasu *vt.* enlarge

hikōjō *n.* 飛行場 airport

hikōki *n.* 飛行機 airplane

hiku *vt.* 引く pull

hikimasu (polite) 引きます

hikui *adj.* 低い low, short

hima *n.* 暇 time, leisure

himitsu *n.* 秘密 secrecy

himitsu no *adj.* 秘密の secret, confidential

himo *n.* 紐 string, cord

hiniku *n.* 皮肉 cynicism, sarcasm

hiniku na *adj.* 皮肉な sarcastic, cynical, caustic

hirogeru *vt.* 拡げる spread out, extend, widen

  hirogemasu (polite) 拡げます

hiroi *adj.* 広い wide, broad

hiru *n.* 昼 daytime, noon

hiru gohan 昼御飯 luncheon

hito *n.* 人 man, person

hitotsu *n.* 一つ one

hiza *n.* 膝 knee, lap

hizuke *n.* 日付 date

hō *n.* 方 direction, way, side

  ippō 一方 one side

hobō *adv.* 方々 here and there, various places

hodo *adv.* 程 about, extent

hōhō *n.* 方法 way, means, method

hohoemi *n.* 微笑 smile

hohoemu *vi.* 微笑む smile

hoka *n.* 外, 他 some other place, somewhere else

hoka no *adj.* 外の other, another, different

hoken *n.* 保険 insurance

hōkō *n.* 方向 direction

hokori *n.* 誇り pride

  hokori to suru 誇とする be proud of

hokori *n.* 埃 dust

hokorobi *n.* 綻び tear, a rip

hokorobiru *vi.* 綻びる be rent, be ripped

homeru *vt.* 褒める praise, admire
　homemasu (polite) 褒めます
hon *n.* 本 book
　hon-bako 本箱 bookcase
　hon-dana 本棚 bookshelf
　hon-ya 本屋 bookshop
hone *n.* 骨 bone
honmono *n.* 本物 genuine, real thing
hontō no *adj.* 本当の real, true
hon no *adv.* ほんの slight, mere, just, only
hon-yaku suru *vt.* 翻訳する translate
　hon-yaku shimasu (polite) 翻訳します
hoshi *n.* 星 star
hoshii *vt.* 欲しい want, desire
hōsō suru *vt. vi.* 放送する broadcast
　hōsōshimasu (polite) 放送します
hōsōkyoku 放送局 broadcasting station
hosoi *adj.* 細い thin, slender, narrow
hoteru *n.* ホテル hotel
hotondo *adv.* 殆んど almost
hyaku *n.* 百 a hundred
hyakushō *n.* 百姓 farmer, peasant
hyōsatsu *n.* 標札 name plate, door plate

I

ichi *n.* 一 one
　ichiji 一時 one o'clock
　ichinichi 一日 one day
　ichijikan 一時間 one hour
　ip pun 一分 one minute
ichiba *n.* 市場 market
ichiban *n.* 一番 the first, most, best

ichido *adv.* 一度 once
Ichi-gatsu *n.* 一月 January
ichiman *n.* 一万 ten thousand
ichiryū no *adj.* 一流の first rate, first class
ie *n.* 家 house, home
igai na *adj.* 意外な unexpected, accidental, surprising
igai ni *adv.* 以外に except, but, other than
ii *adj.* いい fine, good, nice
　ii hito いい人 nice person
iie *adv.* いいえ no
ikaga *adv.* いかが how
　Go-kigen ikaga desu ka?
　御機嫌いかがですか?
　How are you?
ike *n.* 池 pond
ikebana *n.* 生け花 flower arrangement
iken *n.* 意見 opinion, idea, view
ikenai *aux. v.* いけない must not, should not
　sonna koto o shite wa ikanai
　そんなことをしてはいけない
　you must not do such a thing
ikenai *adj.* いけない bad, wrong
　anata ga ikenai あなたがいけない You are in the wrong
iku *vi.* 行く go
　ikimasu (polite) 行きます
ikura *adj. adv.* いくら how much
　Ikura desu ka? いくらですか?
　How much is it?
ikutsu *adj.* いくつ how many? how old?
ima *n.* 今 now, just now
imin *n.* 移民 immigration
imin kyoku 移民局 immigration office
imōto *n.* 妹 younger sister

imōtosan (polite) 妹さん your sister

imushitsu n. 医務室 medical office

inaka n. 田舎 country, countryside

inochi n. 命 life

inshō n. 印象 impression
   daiichi inshō 第一印象 the first impression

inu n. 犬 dog

ippinryōri n. 一品料理 à la carte

irassharu vi. いらっしゃる be (person)
   (*polite form of* **iru**)

irassharu vi. come, call, go
   (*polite expression of* **kuru** *and* **iku**)

iriguchi n. 入口 entrance, way in

iro n. 色 color

iroiro no adj. 色々の various, all sorts of, diverse, different

iru vi. 居る be, exist, reside, stay
   imasu (polite) 居ます

iru vi. 要る want, need, require
   irimasu (polite) 要ります
   iranai 要らない unwanted, unnecessary
   irimasen (polite) 要りません
   Norikae wa irimasen
   乗換えは要りません
   You don't have to change cars.

isha n. 医者 doctor

ishitsubutsu-gakari n. 遺失物係 lost-and-found office

isogashii adj. 忙しい busy

isogu vi. 急ぐ hurry, hasten
   isogimasu (polite) 急ぎます

isoide adv. 急いで in a hurry, hastily

isshōkemmei ni adv. 一生懸命に eagerly, earnestly, hard

issho ni adv. 一緒に together, with, in company with

isu n. 椅子 chair

·**itadaku** vt. 頂く 1. receive, accept, take 2. (food or beverages) take, eat, drink
   itadakimasu (polite) 頂きます

itamu vi. 痛む ache, pain
   itamimasu (polite) 痛みます

itasu vt. 致す do
   itashimasu (polite) 致します

ito n. 糸 thread

itoko n. いとこ cousin

itsu adv. いつ when

itsu made adv. いつまで how long, till when

itsu mo adv. いつも always, whenever, every time, usually

itsutsu n. 五つ five
   itsuka 五日 five days, the fifth day

ittō n. 一等 first class

iu vt. 言う say, remark, tell
   iimasu (polite) 言います

iwa n. 岩 rock

iwaba adv. 言わば so to speak, as it were, in a sense, in short, in a word

J

ja conj. じゃ well, well then, if so, in that case

jama n. 邪魔 hindrance, inconvenience

jama na adj. 邪魔な obstructive, burdensome

jama suru vt. 邪魔する hinder, impede, encumber, bother, disturb
   jamashimasu (polite) 邪魔します
   O-jama desu ka? お邪魔です

か Do I disturb you?

jibun *n.* 自分 self, oneself

jidōsha *n.* 自動車 automobile

jikan *n.* 時間 time, hour

jikanhyō 時間表 timetable

nanji 何時 what time

jiyū *n.* 自由 freedom, liberty

jiyū na *adj.* 自由な free

jiyū ni *adv.* 自由に freely

jochū *n.* 女中 maid

jōdan *n.* 冗談 joke, jest, fun

jōken *n.* 条件 condition, term, stipulation

jōsha *n.* 乗車 boarding (a car, train)

jōzu *n.* 上手 skill, dexterity, adroitness

jōzu na *adj.* 上手な skillful, dexterous

jōzu ni *adv.* 上手に skillfully

Kare wa nan demo jōzu de aru 彼は何でも上手である He is skillful in everything.

jū 十 ten

jūbun na *adj.* 十分な enough, sufficient, plenty

jūbun ni *adv.* 十分に enough, sufficiently, fully

Jū-gatsu *n.* 十月 October

Jūichi-gatsu *n.* 十一月 November

jū-ichi nichi 十一日 eleven days, the eleventh day

junchō na *adj.* 順調な smooth, satisfactory, well, favorable

junchōni *adv.* 順調に smoothly, favorably

Jūni-gatsu *n.* 十二月 December

junkyū *n.* 準急 local express, semi-express

junsui na *adj.* 純粋な pure, genuine

juppun 十分 ten minutes

jūsho *n.* 住所 address

jūsu *n.* ジュース bottled fruit-flavored drinks

jūyō na *adj.* 重要な important

K

ka *particle.* か? (question particle)

kabi *n.* かび mold

kaburu *vt.* 被る put on, wear (hat, cap, etc.)

kaburimasu (polite) 被ります

kachi *n.* 価値 value, worth

kado *n.* 角 corner

kaeru *vi.* 帰 (返) る return, come back

kaerimasu (polite) 帰 (返) ります

kaeru *vt.* 変える change, alter, switch

kaemasu (polite) 変えます

shigoto o kaeru 仕事を変える change one's occupation

kaeru *vt.* 換 (代, 替) える 1. exchange, convert 2. renew 3. substitute, instead of

kaemasu (polite) 換 (代, 替) えます

Nanika hoka no shina to kaete wa ikemasen ka? 何かほかの品と換えてはいけませんか Could I have (take) something else instead?

kaesu *vt.* 返す return, give back

kaeshimasu (polite) 返します

kagaku *n.* 科学 science

shizenkagaku 自然科学 natural science

shizenkagaku hakubutsu-kan 自然科学博物館 natural science museum

kagami *n.* 鏡 mirror

kagayaku *vt.* 輝く shine, glitter

kagayakimasu (polite) 輝きます

kage n. 蔭 shade

kage n. 影 shadow, silhouette

kagetsu n. カ月 months
san-kagetsu 三カ月
three months

kagi n. 鍵 key

kai dan n. 階段 stairs, steps
ikkai 一階 the first floor
nikai 二階 the second floor

kaifuku suru vi. 恢復する
recover, restore, regain
kaifukushimasu (polite) 恢
(回)復します

kaigan n. 海岸 shore, seashore,
beach

kaimono n. 買物 shopping,
purchase

kaisha n. 会社 company, firm
kōkūgaisha 航空会社 airline
funagaisha 船会社
shipping company

kaisūken n. 回数券 book of
tickets

kakaru vi. かかる cost, require,
need
kakarimasu (polite) かかります
(o-) kane ga kakaru お金がか
かる It costs money

kakaru vt. 罹る contract
(a disease), catch (flu)
haien ni kakaru 肺炎に罹る
suffer from pneumonia
kaze o hiku 風邪を引く catch
cold
(**hiku** is used for cold only)

kakitome n. 書留 registered
mail

kaku vt. 書く write
kakimasu (polite) 書きます

kaku vt. 描く paint, draw
kakimasu (polite) 描きます

kakuteru n. カクテル cocktail

kami n. 紙 paper

kamikuzu 紙屑 wastepaper,
scrap paper

kamikuzu kago 紙屑かご
wastepaper basket

kami n. 神 god

kamisama 神さま (this word
commonly used)

kami n. 髪 hair

kami-abura 髪油 hair oil

kamisori n. razor かみそり

kamisori no ha n. かみそりの刃
razor blade

kan n. 缶 can, tin

kankiri 缶切り can opener

kanai n. 家内 my wife

kanari adv. かなり pretty,
fairly, considerably

kanashii adj. 悲しい sad,
sorrowful, woeful, mournful,
tearful, pathetic, unhappy

kane n. 金 money
o-kane (polite) お金

kane n. 鐘 gong, bell

kangae n. 考え 1. thinking,
thought, idea 2. opinion,
view, suggestion, intention
3. discretion, judgment

kangaeru vt. 考える think
kangaemasu (polite) 考えます
kangaete okimashō 考えておき
ましょう I will think about it

kani n. かに crab, lobster

kanjiru vi. 感じる feel, perceive
kanjimasu (polite) 感じます

kanjō n. 勘定 account, bill,
check

kankō n. 観光 sightseeing

kansha n. 感謝 gratitude,
thanks

kansha suru vt. 感謝する
be grateful, thank
kansha shimasu (polite) 感謝

します
kansha itashimasu 感謝
いたし ます I am grateful
kantan na *adj.* 簡単な brief,
simple, plain
kanzen na *adj.* 完全な perfect,
complete, thorough
kao *n.* 顔 face
...**kara** *particle* から from, since,
because, so that
karā fuirumu *n.* カラー フイル
ム color film
karē raisu *n.* カレー ライス
curry rice
kariru *vt.* 借りる borrow, rent
karimasu (polite) 借ります
karui *adj.* 軽い light
(of weight)
kasa *n.* 傘 umbrella
kasanaru *vi.* 重なる be piled up,
accumulate
kasanarimasu (polite) 重なり
ます
(o)-**kashi** *n.* (お)菓子 cake,
sweets, candy
...**kashira** *suf.* かしら I wonder
if, I am afraid of
kasu *vt.* 貸す lend, loan
kashimasu (polite) 貸します
kasumi *n.* 霞 haze, mist
kata *n.* 肩 shoulder
katachi *n.* 形 form, shape,
figure
katai *adj.* 堅い hard, solid,
tough, firm
katamichi *n.* 片道 one way
katarogu *n.* カタログ catalog
katazukeru *vt.* 片付ける
1. put (thing) in order, tidy up,
clear (table) 2. finish 3. settle
(a problem)
katazukemasu (polite) 片付け
ます

kāten *n.* カーテン curtain
katsuretsu *n.* カツレツ (pork)
cutlet
kau *vt.* 買う buy, purchase
kaimasu (polite) 買います
kauntā *n.* カウンター counter
kawa *n.* 川, 河 river
kawa *n.* 皮 skin, leather
kawaii *adj.* 可愛い cute, darling,
charming, lovely, sweet
kawairashii *adj.* 可愛らしい
cute, darling, etc.
kawaisō na *adj.* 可哀そうな
poor, pitiable, pitiful, sad,
unfortunate
kawaku *vi.* 乾く dry
kawakimasu (polite) 乾きます
kawaku *vi.* 渇く feel thirsty
kawakimasu (polite) 渇きます
kawaru *vi.* 変る change
kawarimasu (polite) 変ります
kawarugawaru *adv.* 代る代る
in turn, alternately
kawase *n.* 為替 money order
kawasesōba *n.* 為替相場
exchange rate
gaikoku kawase 外国為替
foreign exchange
kawatta *adj.* 変つた 1. different,
various 2. unusual, extraordinary, odd
Ka-yōbi *n.* 火曜日 Tuesday
kaze *n.* 風 wind, breeze
kaze *n.* 風邪 cold
kaze o hiku 風邪を引く catch
cold
kazu *n.* 数 number
kebakebashii *adj.* けばけばしい
gaudy, garish, flashy, showy,
loud
kechi *n.* けち stinginess
kechi na *adj.* けちな stingy
kechimbō *n.* けちん坊 miser
kega *n.* 怪我 wound, injury,

hurt

kegawa n. 毛皮 fur

keigu n. 敬具 Sincerely yours, Yours truly, Respectfully yours, Faithfully yours

keikaku n. 計画 plan, scheme, plot, program

keikaku suru vt. 計画する plan

keisatsu n. 警察 police, police station

keiyaku n. 契約 contract

keizai n. 経済 economy, finance

kekka n. 結果 result, consequence, outcome

...no kekka の結果 as a result of, in consequence of

kekkō na adj. 結構な good, fine, splendid

kekkō desu 結構です This is good enough

Iie, mō kekkō desu いいえ、もう結構です No, thank you

kekkon n. 結婚 marriage, matrimony

kekkon suru vt. 結婚する get married

kempō n. 憲法 constitution

kenbutsu n. 見物 sightseeing

kenjitsu na adj. 堅実な steady, steadfast, solid, sound, reliable

kenka n. 喧嘩 quarrel, fight, dispute

kenka suru vi. 喧嘩する quarrel

kenkō n. 健康 health

kenkō na adj. 健康な healthy

kenri n. 権利 right, claim, privilege

keredomo conj. けれども but, however

keshiki n. 景色 scenery, view, landscape

kesshite adv. 決して never, by no means, not in the least

kesu vt. 消す 1. put out, extinguish, blow out 2. erase, strike out

keshimasu (polite) 消します

kibatsu na adj. 奇抜な striking, extraordinary

kibishii adj. 厳しい severe, rigorous, strict, stern, intense, harsh

kibo n. 規模 scale, scope

kibō n. 希望 hope, wish, desire, aspiration

kibō suru vt. 希望する hope, desire

kichin to adv. きちんと exactly, accurately, punctually, neatly, tidily, orderly

kichō n. 記帳 registration

kichō na adj. 貴重な precious, valuable, priceless

kichōhin 貴重品 valuables

kieru vi. 消える be blown out, be extinguished, be put out

kiemasu (polite) 消えます

ki ga tsuku vt. 気が付く notice, become aware of, be attentive, find

ki ga tsukimasu (polite) 気が付きます

kigeki n. 喜劇 comedy, farce

ki iro n. 黄色 yellow

ki iro i adj. 黄色い yellow

kiji n. 布地 material, cloth

kiken n. 危険 danger

kiken na adj. 危険な dangerous

kiki n. 危機 crisis

kikkari to adv. きっかりと exactly, punctually, just, sharp

kikō n. 気候 climate

kikoeru vi. 聞える hear, be heard

kikoemasu (polite) 聞こえます

kiku vt. 聞く hear, hear of,

learn, listen to
kikimasu (polite) 聞きます

kimaru vi. 決まる be settled,
be decided, be fixed,
be agreed upon
kimarimasu (polite) 決まり
ます

kimben n. 勤勉 diligence,
industry

kimben na adj. 勤勉な diligent,
industrious, hard-working

kimeru vt. 決める decide, settle,
resolve, determine
kimemasu (polite) 決めます

Kimigayo n. 君が代
the national anthem of Japan

kimochi n. 気持 feeling, mood

kimochi no yoi adj. 気持のよい
pleasant, comfortable,
agreeable

kimono n. 着物 Japanese native
costume

kimyō na adj. 奇妙な strange,
funny, curious, queer, peculiar,
singular

kinaga na adj. 気長な
deliberate, patient

kinen n. 記念 commemoration,
remembrance, memory
kinenhin 記念品 souvenir,
remembrance, memento

kinen suru vt. 記念する
commemorate

kinjo n. 近所 neighborhood
kinjo no adj. 近所の
neighboring, near by
kinjo ni adv. 近所に in the
neighborhood, nearby

kinō n. 昨日 yesterday

kinoko n. きのこ mushroom

kinshi n. 禁止 prohibition
kin-en 禁煙 no smoking
kinseihin 禁制品 prohibited

goods

kinshi suru vt. 禁止する
prohibit

kinu n. 絹 silk

Kin-yōbi n. 金曜日 Friday

kippu n. 切符 ticket

kirai n. 嫌い dislike

kirai na adj. 嫌いな hateful,
distasteful
kiraidesu 嫌いです I dislike it.

kirau vt. 嫌う dislike

kirei na adj. 綺麗な
1. beautiful, pretty, nice
2. clean

kiru 切る vt. cut, slash, shear
kirimasu (polite) 切ります

kiru vt. 着る wear, put on
kimasu (polite) 着ます

kisetsu n. 季節 season
shiki 四季 four seasons

kisha n. 記者 pressman,
journalist, editor, reporter,
correspondent

kisha n. 汽車 (railway) train

kisoku n. 規則 rule, regulation

kita n. 北 north

kitanai adj. 汚い dirty, filthy,
unclean

kitte n. 切手 stamps

kitto adv. きっと surely,
without fail, certainly

kochira pron. こちら this one,
this way, here

kodomo n. 子供 child
kodomo-ra
kodomo-tachi } children

koe n. 声 voice

kōen n. 公園 park, public
garden

kōfuku na adj. 幸福な happy,
blessed, blissful, fortunate,
lucky

kogecha iro n. 焦茶色

dark brown
kogecha iro no *adj.* 焦茶色の
dark brown
kogitte *n.* 小切手 check
  ryokakuyō kogitte 旅客用小
切手 traveler's check
kōgyō *n.* 工業 industry
kōgyō *n.* 興行 performance,
show, exhibition
kōhii *n.* コーヒー coffee
koi *n.* 恋 love
  koibito 恋人 sweetheart
  koibumi 恋文 love letter
kojiki *n.* 乞食 beggar
kōjō *n.* 工場 factory
kōka *n.* 効果 effect
koko, kochira *adv.* ここ, こちら
here
kokonotsu *n.* 九つ nine
kokonoka 九日 nine days,
the ninth day
kokoro *n.* 心 mind, heart, spirit
kōkū *n.* 航空 aviation
kokuden *n.* 国電 government-
operated trains in cities
kōkūgaisha 航空会社 airline
  kōkū yūbin 航空郵便 air mail
kokuren *n.* 国連 the United
Nations (abbreviation of
kokusai rengō 国際連合)
kokusai no *adj.* 国際の international
  kokusa bōekii 国際貿易 international trade
  kokusai rengō 国際連合 the
United Nations
komakai *adj.* 細かい small,
minute, fine, trivial, detailed
komaru *vi.* 困る be troubled by,
be annoyed, be puzzled, be at
a loss
  komarimasu (polite) 困ります
komban *n.* 今晩 this evening
  komban wa 今晩は Good
evening

kondate *n.* 献立 menu
kondo *n.* 今度 this time, now,
next time
konnichi wa 今日は Good
afternoon, Good day
kono *adj.* この this
konogoro *adv.* この頃 lately,
recently, nowadays, these
days
koppu *n.* コップ cup
kore *pron.* これ this, this one
korobasu *vt.* 転ばす roll, throw,
knock (a person) down
  korogasu 転がす
korobu *vi.* 転ぶ fall down,
tumble down
korogaru *vi.* 転がる roll
koshi *n.* 腰 waist, hip
kōshō *n.* 交渉 contact,
connection, negotiation
kōshū *n.* 公衆 the public
kōshū no *adj.* 公衆の public
  kōshū denwa 公衆電話
public telephone
kōsu *n.* コース course
kōsui *n.* 香水 perfume, scent
kotaeru *vt.* 答える reply,
answer
  kotaemasu (polite) 答えます
koto *n.* 事 thing, matter, affair,
fact
kotoba *n.* 言葉 language,
speech, word, term
kotoshi *n.* 今年 this year
kotowaru *vt.* 断る refuse,
decline
  kotowarimasu (polite) 断り
ます
kottōhin *n.* 骨董品 curio,
antique
kowareru *vi.* 毀れる break
  kowaremasu (polite) 毀れます
kowasu *vt.* 毀す break, destroy

kowashimasu (polite) 毀します

kozukai n. 小使 janitor

kozutsumi n. 小包 parcel, package

ku, kyū n. 九 nine

kujū-ku 九十九 ninety-nine

kyūjū 九十 ninety

kubi n. 首, 頸 neck

kubikazari 首飾り necklace

kuchi n. 口 mouth

kuchibeni 口紅 lipstick

kudamono n. 果物 fruit

kudasaru 下さる give, confer, bestow

kudasaimasu (polite) 下さいます

Ku-gatsu n. 九月 September

kumori adj. 曇り cloudy

kūpon n. クーポン coupon

kurabu n. クラブ club

kurai adj. 暗い dark

kurai adv. 位 1. about, more or less 2. as well as

kurasu n. クラス class

kuro n. 黒 black

kuroi adj. 黒い black

kuru vi. 来る come

kimasu (polite) 来ます

kusa n. 草 grass, herb, weed

kushi n. 櫛 comb

kusuri n. 薬 medicine

kusuriya 薬屋 drugstore, pharmacy

kutsu n. 靴 shoes

kutsuhimo 靴ひも shoelaces

kutsushita 靴下 socks

kutsubera 靴べら shoehorn

kutsuzure 靴ずれ shoe sore

kutsurogu 寛ぐ relax, make oneself at home

kutsurogimasu (polite) 寛ぎます

kuwaeru vt. 加える add

kuwashii adj. 詳しい
1. detailed, minute
2. be familiar with

kuzusu vt. くずす change (into small money)

kyabarē n. キャバレー cabaret

kyabin n. キャビン cabin

kyaku n. 客 guest, visitor

o-kyakusama (polite) お客様

kyō n. 今日 today

kyōiku n. 教育 education, instruction

kyōiku suru vt. 教育する educate

kyōju n. 教授 professor

kyōju suru vt. 教授する teach

kyoka n. 許可 permission, approval, authorization

kyoka suru vt. 許可する permit, approve

kyōkai n. 教会 church

kyōkai n. 協会 association, society, institution

kyoku n. 局 bureau, office

kyokutō n. 極東 the Far East

kyōmi n. 興味 interest, taste

kyōmi no aru adj. 興味のある interesting (book), amusing (story), attractive (show)

kyonen n. 去年 last year

kyōryoku n. 協力 cooperation, collaboration

kyōryoku suru vi. 協力する cooperate, collaborate

kyōsai-ka n. 恐妻家 henpecked husband

kyōsanshugi n. 共産主義 communism

kyōsantō 共産党 the Communist Party, the Communists

kyōshi n. 教師 teacher

kyūji n. 給仕 waiter, waitress, office boy
　kyūji o suru vi. 給仕をする wait at table
kyūka n. 休暇 vacation, holiday
　kyūka o toru 休暇をとる take a vacation
kyūkō n. 急行 express
kyūryō n. 給料 pay, wages, salary

M

machi n. 町 town, city
machigaeru vt. 間違える err, mistake
　machigaemasu (polite) 間違えます
machigatte iru vi. 間違っている be mistaken, be wrong, be erroneous
　machigatte imasu (polite) 間違っています
mada adv. まだ still, as yet
made particle 迄 till, until, up to
made ni particle 迄に by, not later than, before
mado n. 窓 window
mae n. 前 the front
mae ni adv. 前に to, before, in front of, ago
mafurā n. マフラー muffler
mai— pref. 毎— every, each
　mainichi 毎日 everyday
　maiban 毎晩 every night
mai suf. 枚 sheet, piece
mairu vi. 参る come, go (humble form of I come)
　mairimasu (polite) 参ります
　Mairimashō ka? 参りましょうか shall we go?
　Jidōsha ga mairimashita 自動車が参りました The car

came
majime na adj. 真面目な serious, earnest, grave, sober, honest, steady
maku vt. 捲く roll, wind
　makimasu (polite) 捲きます
makura n. 枕 pillow
māmarēdo n. マーマレード marmalade
mame n. 豆 beans, peas
mamo naku adv. 間もなく soon, shortly, before long, in a little while
maniau vi. 間に合う 1. be in time for 2. serve the purpose, will do, be of use
　maniaimasu (polite) 間に合います
manikyua n. マニキュア manicure
mannaka n. 真中 middle, center, heart
mannenhitsu n. 万年筆 fountain pen
massāji n. マッサージ massage
massugu adv. 真直ぐ straight
mata adv. また 1. again, once more 2. too, also, as well
mata wa conj. または or
mataseru vt. 待たせる keep one waiting
　matasemasu (polite) 待たせます
　Dōmo o-matase itashimashita どうもお待たせ致しました I am sorry to have kept you waiting.
matchi n. マッチ match
　matchi o surimasu マッチをすります lights a match
matsu vt. 待つ 1. wait for, await 2. expect, anticipate, look forward to

machimasu (polite) 待ちます

machiaishitsu n. 待合室 waiting room

mattaku adv. 全く quite, entirely, completely, wholly, utterly

mawaru vi. 回る turn, go round, revolve

  mawarimasu (polite) 回ります

  Kuruma ga mawaru 車が回る Wheel turns

mawasu vt. 回す 1. turn, revolve, rotate 2. forward (letter), hand around

  mawashimasu (polite) 回します

  Kuruma o mawasu 車を回す Turn the wheel

mayou vi. 迷う be perplexed, be bewildered, be at a loss

  mayoimasu (polite) 迷います

mazeru vt. 混ぜる mix, blend, mingle

  mazemasu (polite) 混ぜます

mazushii adj. 貧しい poor, needy, indigent, destitute

me n. 目 eye

me n. 芽 sprout

megane n. 眼鏡 eye glasses, spectacles

mei n. 姪 niece

meishi n. 名刺 calling card, visiting card

meishin n. 迷信 superstition

meisho n. 名所 place of interest

meisho kyūseki n. 名所旧跡 picturesque and historical sites

meiwaku n. 迷惑 trouble

  meiwaku o kakeru 迷惑をかける put one to trouble, cause one inconvenience

meiwaku suru 迷惑する be troubled, get into trouble. be annoyed

  meiwaku shimasu (polite) 迷惑します

meiwaku na adj. 迷惑な troublesome

mekata n. 目方 weight

mendō n. 面倒 trouble

  mendō o kakeru 面倒をかける give a person trouble

  Go-mendō o o-kakeshima-shite sumimasen ご面倒をおかけしましてすみません I am sorry to trouble you

mendō na adj. 面倒な difficult, troublesome, annoying

  Mendō na koto ni narima-shita 面倒なことになりました The matter has become complicated This is going to be tough

menkai n. 面会 interview, meeting

menshita adj. 面した facing

mensuru vi. 面する to face, look out on, front on

merodii n. メロディー melody

meshiagaru 召し上がる eat, drink, help oneself to eat or drink

  meshiagarimasu (polite) 召し上がります

  Dōzo o-kashi o meshiagatte kudasai どうぞお菓子を召し上がって下さい Please help yourself to the cake

mētā n. メーター meter (for a taxi)

metoru n. メートル meter

mezurashii adj. 珍らしい

1. rare, uncommon 2. curious, strange

michi *n.* 道 street, road, way

midori *n.* 緑 green, verdure

midori no *adj.* 緑の green

mieru *vi* 見える is visible, can be seen

   miemasu (polite) 見えます

migaku *vt.* 磨く 1. polish, brush up, shine 2. cultivate (one's mind)

   migakimasu (polite) 磨きます

   Kutsu o migaite kudasai 靴を磨いて下さい Please shine my shoes

migi *n.* 右 right

migi gawa 右側 right side

miharashi *n.* 見晴らし view, prospect, outlook

mihon *n.* 見本 sample, specimen, pattern

mijikai *adj.* 短かい short, brief

mikan *n.* 蜜柑 mandarin orange, tangerine

mikka 三日 *n.* three days, the third day

mimi *n.* 耳 ear

mina 皆, **minna** みんな *n.* all, everything, everyone

   Minna de ikura desu ka? 皆でいくらですか How much in all?

   Minasan, sayonara 皆さんさよなら Goodbye, everybody

minami *n.* 南 south

minato *n.* 港 harbor, port

minshushugi *n.* 民主主義 democracy

miru *vt.* 見る to see, to look

   mimasu (polite) 見ます

misairu *n.* ミサイル missile

mise *n.* 店 shop, store

miseru *vt.* 見せる show, exhibit,

demonstrate, display

   misemasu (polite) 見せます

mitomeru *vt.* 認める recognize, acknowledge, admit

   mitomemasu (polite) 認めます

mitsukeru *vt.* 見付ける find, discover, detect

   mitsukemasu (polite) 見付けます

mitsumori *n.* 見積り estimate

mittsu *n.* 三つ three

mizu *n.* 水 water

   mizugi 水着 bathing suit

   mizuiro *n.* 水色 pale blue

   mizuumi *n.* 湖 lake

mo も **mo mata** も又 *particle* 1. also, too, as well 2. either, neither

mō *adv.* もう 1. now 2. soon, before long, shortly 3. already

mochiron *adv.* 勿論 of course, needless to say

modoru *vi.* 戻る return, come back

   modorimasu (polite) 戻ります

moeru *vi.* 燃える burn

   moemasu (polite) 燃えます

mō ichido *adv.* もう一度 once more, again

   mō ichido itte kudasai もう一度云つて下さい I beg your pardon

moji *n.* 文字 letter, character

mokuteki *n.* 目的 aim, object, objective, purpose, end, intention

Moku-yōbi *n.* 木曜日 Thursday

mon *n.* 門 gate, gateway

mondai *n.* 問題 question, problem

morau *vt.* 貰う receive, take, get

   moraimasu (polite) 貰います

moshi *conj.* 若し if, provided, supposing

mōshikomi *n.* 申し込み 1. application 2. offer, proposal

mōshikomu *vt.* 申込む propose, offer, apply for
mōshikomimasu (polite) 申込みます

moshi moshi *int.* もしもし Hello! I say!

mōsu *vt.* 申す say (*humble form of* iu)
mōshimasu (polite) 申します
...to mōshimasu と申します It is called that

motenasu *vt.* もてなす entertain, treat
motenashimasu (polite) もてなします

motsu *vt.* 持つ have, carry, hold
mochimasu (polite) 持ちます

motto *adv.* もっと more, much, longer

mottomo *adv.* 最も most, extremely, exceedingly, supremely

moyasu *vt.* 燃やす to burn
moyashimasu (polite) 燃やします

moyori no *adj.* 最寄の nearest, neighboring, adjacent, in the vicinity

muda na *adj.* 無駄な wasteful, useless, futile, unavailing

mugi *n.* 麦 wheat, barley, oats, rye

muika 六日 six days, the sixth day

muku *vi.* 向く turn, look
mukimasu (polite) 向きます

mune *n.* 胸 chest, breast, bust

mura *n.* 村 village

murasaki *n.* 紫 purple

muri na *adj.* 無理な unjust, unreasonable, impossible

mushi *n.* 虫 insect, bug, worm

mushiatsui *adj.* 蒸し暑い sultry, muggy, stuffy

musubu *vt.* 結ぶ tie, knot, make (a contract), form (friendship) conclude (a treaty)
musubimasu (polite) 結びます

musume *n.* 娘 daughter

mutonjaku na *adj.* 無頓着な indifferent, nonchalant, careless

muttsu *n.* 六つ six

muzukashii *adj.* むずかしい difficult, hard, troublesome

N

na *n.* 名 name

nadakai *adj.* 名高い famous

nado *suf.* 等 et cetera

nagai *adj.* 長い long, lengthy, prolonged

nagame *n.* 眺め view, prospect, scenery

nagameru *vt.* 眺める look at, gaze at, stare at
nagamemasu (polite) 眺めます

nagara *conj.* ながら while

nagareru *vi.* 流れる stream, flow, run
nagaremasu (polite) 流れます

nagasa *n.* 長さ length, measure

naifu *n.* ナイフ knife

najimi *n.* 馴染 familiarity, acquaintance, intimacy
najimi no *adj.* 馴染の familiar

naka *n.* 中 inside, interior

nakereba *conj.* なければ if not, unless, but for, were it not for

nakigoto n. 泣き言 complaint, whining, grumbling

nakigoto o iu vi. 泣き言を言う complain

naku vi. 泣く (human being) cry, weep

nakimasu (polite) 泣きます

naku vi. 鳴く, 啼く (birds, animals) cry, bark, yelp, coo, sing

nakimasu (polite) 鳴きます, 啼きます

nakunaru vi. なくなる be lost, be gone, be missing, run short (e. g. money)

nakunarimasu (polite) なくなります

nakunaru vi. 亡くなる die, pass away

nakusu 失くす **nakusuru** vt. 失くする lose, be out of, miss

nakushimasu (polite) 失くします

nama adj. なま raw, uncooked

namanie no adj. 生煮えの half-cooked, rare

namayake no adj. 生焼けの half-roasted, half-baked, rare

namae n. 名前 name

namakeru vi. 怠ける be idle, be lazy

namakemasu (polite) 怠けます

namanurui adj. 生温い lukewarm

nami n. 波 wave, surf, ripple

namida n. 涙 tear

nanatsu n. 七つ seven

nandaka adv. 何だか somewhat, somehow, for some reason or other

nandemo n. 何でも any, anything, whatever

nani n. 何 what

nanoka 七日 seven days, the seventh day

naoru vi. 直(治)る 1. be mended, be fixed 2. get well (from illness), recover 3. be corrected

naorimasu (polite) 直(治)ります

naosu vt. 直(治)す 1. mend, repair, fix up, 2. correct, reform

naoshimasu (polite) 直(治)します

naru vi. なる become, get, be, make oneself

narimasu (polite) なります

naru vi. 鳴る sound, ring, toll, strike

narimasu (polite) 鳴ります

narubeku adv. なるべく 1. as...as possible, as...as one can 2. if possible

naruhodo adv. なるほど indeed

naruhodo int. なるほど I see, indeed, really, to be sure

nasaru なさる do (polite form of **suru**)

nasaimasu (polite) なさいます

nashi n. 梨 pear (fruit)

natsu n. 夏 summer

natsukashii adj. 懐かしい longed for, of dear memory, dear

nawa n. 縄 rope

naze adv. なぜ why, for what reason, on what ground

nedan n. 値段 price

negau vt. 願う desire, wish, hope, beg, deplore

negaimasu (polite) 願います

neko n. 猫 cat, puss, kitten

nekutai n. ネクタイ necktie

nemuri n. 眠り sleep

nemuru vi. 眠る sleep, fall

asleep, take a nap
nemurimasu (polite) 眠ります
neru vi. 寝る sleep, go to bed,
be in bed, lie down
   nemasu (polite) 寝ます
netsu n. 熱 1. fever,
temperature 2. heat
neuchi n. 値打 value, worth,
merit, price
ni n. 二 two
   nijū-ni 二十二 twenty-two
...**ni** particle. ...に in, at, to, for
niau vi. 似合う be suitable, fit,
suit, become
   niaimasu (polite) 似合います
Nichi-Bei adj. 日米 Japan and
the United States, Japan and
America
   Nichi-Bei kawase sōba 日米
為替相場 yen-dollar rate
   Nichi-Bei no 日米の
Japanese-American
Nichi-yōbi n. 日曜日 Sunday
nidome adv. 二度目 for the
second time
Ni-gatsu n. 二月 February
nigeru vi. 逃げる escape,
get away, flee
   nigemasu (polite) 逃げます
nigiru vt. 握る grasp, hold,
seize, clasp
   nigirimasu (polite) 握ります
nigiyaka na adj. 賑やか
1. lively, cheerful, gay
2. noisy
nijuppun 二十分 twenty minutes
nikai n. 二回 twice, two times
nikki n. 日記 diary
niku n. 肉 meat
nimotsu n. 荷物 baggage,
luggage
ningyō n 人形 doll
Nippon or **Nihon** n. 日本 Japan

Nihongo 日本語 Japanese
niru vi. 似る resemble, be alike,
be similar to
   nimasu (polite) 似ます
   nite iru vi. 似ている
be similar to, resemble
niryū n. 二流 second rate,
second class
   niryū no adj. 二流の second
rate, second class
nishi n. 西 west
nitō n. 二等 second class
niwa n. 庭 garden, courtyard
...**niwa** particle. ...には in, for,
to
...**no** particle. ...の of, in, at,
for
nobasu vt. 延ばす put off,
postpone
   nobashimasu (polite) 延ばし
ます
nobasu vt. 伸ばす lengthen,
stretch
   nobashimasu (polite) 伸ばし
ます
nobiru vi. 伸(延)びる extend,
stretch, spread, be postponed
   nobimasu (polite) 伸(延)びます
...**node** particle. ...ので
since, because, so that
nodo n. 喉 throat
   nodo ga kawakimasu 喉がか
わきます feel thirsty
nōgyō n. 農業 agriculture,
farming
nohara n. 野原 field, plain
nokoru vi. 残る remain, stay,
be left
   nokorimasu (polite) 残ります
nokosu vt. 残す leave, save
   nokoshimasu (polite) 残します
nomu vt. 飲む drink
   nomimasu (polite) 飲みます

nomimono *n.* 飲物 beverage

...no ni *particle.* ...のに though, although, in spite of, while, in order to

nori *n.* 糊 starch, paste

noriireru *vi.* 乗り入れる drive into, ride into, extend
noriiremasu (polite) 乗り入れます

norikae *n.* 乗換 (transportation) change, transfer

norikaeru *vt.* 乗換える change (train), transfer

noriki *n.* 乗気 eagerness, enthusiasm
noriki ni naru 乗気になる take an interest in, has a zeal for, become enthusiastic

noru *vi.* 乗る ride, board, take (train)
norimasu (polite) 乗ります

nōryoku *n.* 能力 ability, faculty, capacity

nuu *vt.* 縫う sew, stitch
nuimasu (polite) 縫います

nugu *vt.* 脱ぐ take off, put off
nugimasu (polite) 脱ぎます

nukeru *vi.* 抜ける come off, slip out, fall off
nukemasu (polite) 抜けます

nuku *vt.* 抜く draw out, pull out, extract, remove
nukimasu (polite) 抜きます

nureru *vi.* 濡れる get wet
nuremasu (polite) 濡れます

nurui *adj.* ぬるい lukewarm, tepid

O

...o *particle.* ...を direct object (*postposition*)

o- *pref.* お—(honorific prefix)

o-ainikusama おあいにくさま sorry, unfortunately

ochiru *vi.* 落ちる fall, come down, drop
ochimasu (polite) 落ちます

odorokasu *vt.* 驚かす to surprise, to frighten, to astonish
odorokashimasu (polite) 驚かします

odoroku *vi.* 驚く be surprised, be astonished, be frightened
odorokimasu (polite) 驚きます

ōfuku *n.* 往復 round-trip

ōi *adj.* 多い lots of, plenty of

oide *n.* お出で coming, going, being
Oide kudasai お出で下さい please come
Dochira e oide desu ka? どちらへお出ででですか Where are you going?
Otōsama wa oide desu ka? お父様はお出ででですか Is your father at home?

oishii *adj.* おいしい delicious, tasty

okashii *adj.* おかしい amusing, funny

okiru *vi.* 起きる get up, rise
okimasu (polite) 起きます

okonai *n.* 行い action, act, deed, conduct, deportment, behavior, demeanor, manners

okoru *vi.* 怒る get angry, be enraged, be offended, lose one's temper
okorimasu (polite) 怒ります

okoru *vi.* 起る occur, happen, arise, turn up
okorimasu (polite) 起ります

okosu *vt.* 起す raise up, set upright, give rise to, wake up
okoshimasu (polite) 起します

oku *vt.* 置く place, put, lay
okimasu (polite) 置きます

okureru *vi.* 遅れる be late,
be delayed
okuremasu (polite) 遅れます

okuru *vt.* 送る send, remit,
dispatch
okurimasu (polite) 送ります

okusama 奥様 **okusan** *n.* 奥さん
madam, wife, Mrs.
Watanabe san no okusama
渡辺さんの奥様
Mrs. Watanabe

o-me ni kakaru お目にかかる
see, meet, has the honor of
meeting (polite expression)
o-me ni kakarimasu (polite)
お目にかかります

o-me ni kakeru お目にかける
show, present, submit
(polite expression)
o-me ni kakemasu (polite) お
目にかけます

Omedetō gozaimasu
おめでとうございます
Congratulations !

omoi *adi.* 重い heavy, weighty

omoidasaseru *vt.* 思い出させる
be reminded of, remind one of
omoidasasemasu (polite) 思い
出させます

omoidasu *vi.* 思い出す recollect,
remind, recall
omoidashimasu (polite) 思い
出します

omo na *adj.* 主な main, chief,
leading, principal

omoshiroi *adj.* 面白い
interesting, pleasant, delightful, entertaining, amusing,
funny

omou *vt.* 思う 1. think, consider
2. imagine, suppose 3. believe,
4. feel
omoimasu (polite) 思います

omuretsu *n.* オムレツ omelet

onaji *adj.* 同じ same, identical

o-negai shimasu お願いし
ます I want, Give me, please.
Please do

ongaku *n.* 音楽 music
ongakkai 音楽会 concert

onna 女 woman, female
onna no ko 女の子 girl

onsen *n.* 温泉 hot spring, spa

oriru *vi.* 降りる step down,
descend, get off
orimasu (polite) 降ります

orizume *n.* 折詰 food packed in
a chip box

oru (=**iru**) *vi.* 居る be, stay
(humble expression)
orimasu (polite) 居ります
Chichi wa uchi ni orimasu
父は家に居ります Father is
at home

oshieru *vt.* 教える teach, tell,
instruct, show
oshiemasu (polite) 教えます

o-shiroi *n.* お白粉 face powder

osoi *adj.* 遅い late, behind time

osoraku *adv.* 恐らく perhaps,
probably, maybe

osore irimasu 恐れ入ります
Excuse me, Pardon me,
Thank you

o-tearai *n.* お手洗い toilet,
washroom (polite expression)

oto *n.* 音 sound, noise

otoko *n.* 男 man, male
otoko no ko 男の子 boy

otosu *vt.* 落す drop, let fall
otoshimasu (polite) 落します

ototoi *n.* 一昨日 the day before
yesterday

ototoshi 一昨年 the year before,

last year

owaru *vi.* 終る end, close, expire, result in, complete, conclude

   owarimasu (polite) 終ります

oya *n.* 親 parent

oyogu *vi.* 泳ぐ swim

   oyogimasu (polite) 泳ぎます

oyoso *adv.* およそ about, nearly, roughly, around

P

pan *n.* パン bread

panfuretto *n.* パンフレット pamphlet

parasoru *n.* パラソル parasol

pāsento *n.* パーセント percent

pasupōto *n.* パスポート passport

   ryoken 旅券 passport

pedaru *n.* ペダル pedal

pēji *n.* ページ page

pinku *n.* ピンク pink

pinku no *adj.* ピンクの pink

pondo *n.* ポンド pound

puremiamu *n.* プレミアム premium

puresu *n.* プレス press

purezento *n.* プレゼント gift, present

R

raikyaku *n.* 来客 visitor, guest

rainen *n.* 来年 next year

raishū *n.* 来週 next week

rajio *n.* ラヂオ radio

raketto *n.* ラケット racket

...rashii *aux.* ...らしい it seems like, probably, it appears

   suf. be like, be worthy of

   shinshi rashii 紳士らしい gentlemanly

rein-kōto *n.* レインコート

raincoat

rekishi *n.* 歴史 history, annals, chronicle

renraku *n.* 連絡 connection, junction, communication, correspondence, liaison, contact

renraku suru *vt.* 連絡する to communicate

   renraku shimasu (polite) 連絡します

renshū *n.* 練習 training, practice, exercise, drill

   renshū suru 練習する practice, drill

renzu *n.* レンズ lens

resutoran *n.* レストラン restaurant

rippa na *adj.* 立派な fine, handsome, splendid, magnificent

riyū *n.* 理由 reason, cause, grounds, motive, pretext

rōka *n.* 廊下 corridor, passage

roketto *n.* ロケット rocket

roku *n.* 六 six

   rokujū-roku 六十六 sixty-six

Roku-gatsu *n.* 六月 June

Rōmaji *n.* ローマ字 Romanization

rusu ni suru 留守にする be absent from, be out

   rusu ni shimasu (polite) 留守にします

ryōhō *n.* 両方 both

ryōhō no *adj.* 両方の both

ryōji 領事 consul

   ryōji-kan *n.* 領事館 consulate

   sōryōji 総領事 Consul General

ryokan *n.* 旅館 inn

ryokō *n.* 旅行 trip, travel, journey

ryōri *n.* 料理 cooking, cookery,

dish, food

ryōri suru *vi.* 料理する cook

ryōshin *n.* 良心 conscience

ryōshin *n.* 両親 parents

ryūgaku *n.* 留学 studying abroad

ryūgaku suru *vi.* 留学する study abroad

  ryūgaku shimasu (polite) 留学します

ryūkō *n.* 流行 fashion, vogue

S

sābisu *n.* サービス service

sadō *n.* 茶道 tea ceremony

sagasu *vt.* 探す look for, seek, search

  sagashimasu (polite) 探します

saifu *n.* 財布 purse

saigo *n.* 最後 the last, the end

saigo no *adj.* 最後の last, final

saigo ni *adv.* 最後に lastly, finally

saijitsu *n.* 祭日 national holidays

sainō *n.* 才能 talent, ability

saisho *n*, 最初 first, beginning, outset

saisho no *adj.* 最初の first

saisho ni *adv.* 最初に in the first place, at first

saishū *n.* 最終 the last

saishū no *adj.* 最終の last

sajiki *n.* 桟敷 box seats

saka *n.* 坂 slope, hill

saka *n.* 茶菓 refreshments

sakana *n.* 魚 fish

sakana *n.* 肴 side fish, hors d'œuvre

sake *n.* 酒 rice wine

sambun *n.* 散文 prose, prose writings

sampatsu *n.* 散髪 hair cut

sampatsu suru *v.* 散髪する have one's hair cut

sampo *n.* 散歩 walk, stroll, lounge, promenade, turn

sampo suru *v.* 散歩する take a walk

samui *adj.* 寒い cold, chilly

...san *suf.* さん Mr., Mrs., Miss

san *n.* 三 three

  sanjū-san 三十三 thirty-three

San-gatsu *n.* 三月 March

sangyō *n.* 産業 industry

sanrinsha *n.* 三輪車 tricycle

sansei *n.* 賛成 approval, agreement

sansei suru *vt.* 賛成する approve, agree, support, vote for

  sansei shimasu (polite) 賛成します

santō *n.* 三等 third class

sara *n.* 皿 plate, dish, platter

sarainen *n.* 再来年 the year after next

saraishū *n.* 再来週 the week after next

sarani *adv.* 更に in addition, moreover

sasu *vt.* 指す point out, indicate, point to

  sashimasu (polite) 指します

satō *n.* 砂糖 sugar

sayonara *int.* さよなら Goodbye

sebiro *n.* 背広 (men's) suit

seifu *n.* 政府 government

seiji *n.* 政治 government, administration, politics, political affairs

seikaku *n.* 性格 character

seinen *n.* 青年 youth

seisan *n.* 生産 production, manufacture

seisan suru vt. 生産する produce
　seisan shimasu (polite) 生産します

seishin n. 精神 soul, spirit, mind

seishitsu n. 性質 nature, character, disposition, temperament

Seiyō n. 西洋 the West, the Occident

sekai n. 世界 world

seki n. 席 seat

sekinin n. 責任 responsibility, duty, obligation

sekken n. 石鹼 soap

semai adj. 狭い narrow

sen n. 千 a thousand

sen n. 線 line

senaka n. 背中 back

senden n. 宣伝 propaganda, publicity

sengetsu n. 先月 last month

sen-i n. 繊維 textile, fiber

sensei n. 先生 teacher, instructor, doctor

senshitsu n. 船室 stateroom, cabin

senshū n. 先週 last week

sensō n. 戦争 war, battle, combat, hostilities, warfare

sentaku n. 洗濯 laundry washing, wash

sentaku suru vt. 洗濯する wash
　sentaku shimasu (polite) 洗濯します

setsu n. 節 season, time, occasion
　sono setsu その節 at that time, on that occasion

setsumei n. 説明 explanation

setsumei suru vt. 説明する explain, elucidate, illustrate

setsumei shimasu (polite) 説明します

setsuyaku n. 節約 economy, frugality,

setsuyaku suru vi. 節約する save, economize, cut down
　setsuyaku shimasu (polite) 節約します

setto n. セット set (for hair-dressing)

shakai n. 社会 society, public

shakkin n. 借金 debt, loan

shakkin suru vt. 借金する fall into debt
　shakkin shimasu (polite) 借金します

shashin n. 写真 picture, photo

shawā n. シャワー shower (or bath)

shi n. 詩 poetry, poem

shi n. 四 four
　shijū (=**yonjū**) 四十 forty

shi n. 市 city

shiageru vt. 仕上げる finish, complete, accomplish
　shiagemasu (polite) 仕上げます

shiai n. 試合 game, match, bout, tournament

shibai n. 芝居 show, play, drama

shibaraku adv. 暫く for a while

shichi n. 七 seven

Shichi-gatsu n. 七月 July

shichiji 七時 seven o'clock

shichijū-shichi 七十七 seventy-seven

shichū n. シチュー stew

shiden n. 市電 streetcar

Shi-gatsu n. 四月 April

shigoto n. 仕事 work, task, employment, occupation, job

shiharau vt. 支払う pay, defray,

discharge

shiharaimasu (polite) 支払います

shihon *n.* 資本 capital, funds

shiji *n.* 支持 support, backing

shiji suru *vt.* 支持する support, maintain, uphold, endorse

shiji shimasu (polite) 支持します

shijō *n.* 市場 market

shijō kachi 市場価値 market value

shikaku *n.* 資格 qualification, competency, eligibility, capacity

shikashi *conj.* しかし but, however

shikin *n.* 資金 funds, capital, money

shikkari shita *adj.* しっかりした firm, resolute, sturdy, sound

shikkari to *adv.* しっかりと firmly, tightly, securely, fast, strongly

shikki *n.* 漆器 lacquer ware

shikujiru *vi.* しくじる fail, make a blunder, make a mistake

shikujirimasu (polite) しくじります

shima *n.* 島 island

shimajima 島々 islands

shimbō suru *vi.* 辛抱する be patient, endure

shimbō shimasu (polite) 辛抱します

shimbun *n.* 新聞 newspaper, press

shimeppoi *adj.* 湿っぽい damp, humid, wet

shimeru *vt.* 締める tie, bind, tighten, shut, close

shimemasu (polite) 締めます

shimpai *n.* 心配 worry, trouble, anxiety, apprehension

shimpai suru *vi.* 心配する worry

shimpai shimasu (polite) 心配します

shinai *vt.* しない don't, do not

shimasen (polite) しません

shinjiru *vt.* 信じる believe, trust, be confident

shinjimasu (polite) 信じます

shinju *n.* 真珠 pearl

shinobu *vt.* 忍ぶ bear, endure, put up with, persevere

shinobimasu (polite) 忍びます

shinsetsu *n.* 親切 kindness, goodness

shinsetsu na *adj.* 親切な kind, good, friendly, cordial

shinshi *n.* 紳士 gentleman

shinu *vi.* 死ぬ die, pass away

shinimasu (polite) 死にます

shin-yō *n.* 信用 credit, reputation, trust, credence, confidence

shin-yō suru *vt.* 信用する trust

shio *n.* 塩 salt

shippai suru *vi.* 失敗する fail, be unsuccessful, go wrong

shippai shimasu (polite) 失敗します

shiraberu *vt.* 調べる investigate, check up, examine, inquire into

shirabemasu (polite) 調べます

shirase *n.* 知らせ report, notice, information

shiriai *n.* 知合い acquaintance

shiro *n.* 白 white

shiroi *adj.* 白い white

shirushi *n.* 印 brand, sign, mark

shisatsu *n.* 視察 inspection,

survey, examination

shisatsu suru vt. 視察する inspect

shita n. 下 under, below

shitei n. 指定 designation

shiteiseki 指定席 reserved seats

shitei suru vt. 指定する appoint, designate

...shite kudasai ...して下さい please do..., will you please do...

shiten n. 支店 (an office, shop, etc.) branch

shitogeru vt. 仕遂げる finish, complete, carry out, accomplish, achieve

　shitogemasu (polite) 仕遂げます

shitsubō n. 失望 disappointment

shitsubō suru vi. 失望する be disappointed, be disheartened

shitsumon n. 質問 question, inquiry, query

shitsumon suru vi. 質問する ask a question

shitsurei shimasu 失礼します Excuse me, Pardon me

shizen n. 自然 nature

shizen no adj. 自然の natural

shizen ni adv. 自然に naturally

shizuka na adj. 静かな quiet

shō n. 省 ministry

　Rōdōshō 労働省 Ministry of Labor

　Mombusho 文部省 Ministry of Education

shōbai n. 商売 trade, business

shōchi suru vt. 承知する consent, agree, accede to, comply with

　shōchi shimasu (polite) 承知

shōgyō n. 商業 commerce, trade

shōhin n. 商品 goods, commodity, merchandise

shōjiki n. 正直 honesty, uprightness

shōjiki na adj. 正直な honest, upright, square, straight-forward

shōjiki ni adv. 正直に honestly

shōkai n. 紹介 introduction, recommendation

shōkai suru vt. 紹介する introduce, recommend

shokudō n. 食堂 dining room

shokudōsha 食堂車 dining car

shokugyō n. 職業 occupation, business, employment

shokuji n. 食事 meal, diet

shokuyoku n. 食欲 appetite, relish

shomei n. 署名 signature

shomei suru vt. 署名する sign one's name, affix one's signature

shōmei n. 証明 proof, evidence, testimony

shōmei suru vt. 証明する prove, verify, certify

shōnin n. 商人 merchant, dealer, trader, shopkeeper

shōnin n. 承認 approval, recognition, agreement, consent

shōnin suru vt. 承認する approve, recognize, acknowledge, admit

shōsai n. 詳細 details, particulars

shōsai na adj. 詳細な detailed, full, circumstantial, minute

shōsai ni adv. 詳細に in detail, minutely

shōsen n. 省線 government-operated trains in cities

shōshō *adv.* 少々 just a moment, just a little

shōtai *n.* 招待 invitation

shōtai suru *vt.* 招待する invite
shōtai shimasu (polite) 招待
します

shōtotsu *n.* 衝突 collision, impact, clash, conflict, quarrel

shōtotsu suru *vt.* 衝突する collide with

shōyu *n.* 醤油 soy sauce

shufu *n.* 首府 capital, metropolis

shujin *n.* 主人 husband, master

shujutsu *n.* 手術 operation, surgery

shūkan *n.* 習慣 habit, custom, practice

shūkan *n.* 週間 a week
kono isshukan この一週間
in (during) the past week

shukka *n.* 出荷 shipment

shukka suru *vt.* 出荷する ship, forward

shūkyō *n.* 宗教 religion, faith

shumi *n.* 趣味 hobby, taste, interest

shuppatsu *n.* 出発 departure, start

shuppatsu suru *vi.* 出発する depart (from)

shurui *n.* 種類 kind, sort, variety, type, classification

shusshi *n.* 出資 investment, contribution

shussi suru *vi.* 出資する invest

shūten *n.* 終点 terminal

shūzen *n.* 修繕 repair, mending, renovation

shūzen suru *vt.* 修繕する repair, mend

sō *adv.* そう that's right

Sō desu ka そうですか
Is that so?

Sō desu ne そうですね
Let me see

sochira *pron.* そちら there

sōdan *n.* 相談 consultation, talk

sōdan suru *vi.* 相談する consult, confer

sode *n.* 袖 sleeve

sōji *n.* 掃除 cleaning

sōji suru *vt.* 掃除する clean

soko *n.* そこ there (that place)

soko *n.* 底 bottom, sole

sokutatsu *n.* 速達 special delivery

sono *adj.* その that
sono mama そのまま
as it is, as it stands, intact

sora *n.* 空 sky

sore *pron.* それ it, that one

sorekara *conj.* それから and, then, after that, since then

soretomo *conj.* それとも or

soshiki *n.* 組織 organization, structure, constitution, system

soshite *conj.* そして and, then, now

sotchoku na *adj.* 卒直な frank, plain, candid, outspoken, straightforward

soto *n.* 外 outside

sōtō na *adj.* 相当な good (income), fair

sōtō ni *adv.* 相当に fairly, quite

subarashii *adj.* すばらしい wonderful, grand, great, splendid, magnificent

...sugi *suf.* ...過ぎ *past* (the hour)

sugu ni *adv.* 直ぐに immediately, instantly, at once, right away, soon, easily, readily

suiei *n.* 水泳 swimming

Sui-yōbi *n,* 水曜日 Wednesday

sukēto *n.* スケート skating

suki desu *vi.* すきです like, be fond of

suki na *adj.* すきな fond (of)

sukkari *adv.* すっかり all, quite, completely, entirely, thoroughly, perfectly

sukoa *n.* スコア score

sukoshi *adv.* 少し a little, a few, some

suna *n.* 砂 sand

sunao na *adj.* 素直な obedient, meek, gentle

supōtsu *n.* スポーツ sports

sūpu *n.* スープ soup

supūn *n.* スプーン spoon

suru *vt.* する do
  shimasu (polite) します
  Dō shimashō ka? どうしましょうか What shall I do?

suru *vt.* 為る (する) try, attempt, act, do
  shimasu (polite) します

suru tsumori de aru する積りである expect to do, intend to do
  suru tsumori desu (polite) する積りです

suteki na *adj.* 素敵な wonderful, splendid, great, remarkable

sutēki *n.* ステーキ steak

suteru *vt.* 捨てる 1. throw away, dump 2. abandon, give up
  sutemasu (polite) 捨てます

sutokkingu *n.* ストッキング stockings

sutoraiki *n.* ストライキ strike

suwaru *vi.* 坐る sit down
  suwarimasu (polite) 坐ります

suzushii *adj.* 涼しい cool

T

ta *n.* 田 rice field

tabako *n.* タバコ cigarettes, tobacco

taberu *vt.* 食べる eat, take (food)
  tabemasu (polite) 食べます

tabitabi *adv.* たびたび many times, frequently, repeatedly

tabun *adv.* 多分 perhaps, probably, presumably, maybe

tachiyoru *vi.* 立ち寄る drop in, stop by, visit, call upon
  tachiyorimasu (polite) 立ち寄ります

tada *adv.* ただ only, just, merely

tadaima *int.* 只今 now, just now, in a minute

...tai *aux.* ...たい wish to..., ...hope to, ...should like to...
  ...tai desu (polite) たいです
  ...tai no desu (polite) たいのです

tada no *adj.* 只の free, free of charge

tadashii *adj.* 正しい right, proper, honest, correct

taido *n.* 態度 attitude, manner, demeanor, bearing

Taiheiyō *n.* 太平洋 the Pacific Ocean

taihen na *adj.* 大変な serious, grave, difficult, wonderful, very much

taipuraitā *n.* タイプライター typewriter

Taiseiyō *n.* 太西洋 the Atlantic Ocean

Kita-Taiseiyō Jōyaku Kikō 北太西洋条約機構 the North Atlantic Treaty Organization

taisetsu na *adj.* 大切な great, important, valuable, precious

taishi *n.* 大使 ambassador

taishikan *n.* 大使館 embassy
　Amerika Taishikan アメリカ大使館 American Embassy

taiyō *n.* 太陽 sun

taizai *n.* 滞在 stay, sojourn

taizai suru *vi.* 滞在する stay

taka *n.* 鷹 hawk

takai *adj.* 高い high, tall, loud, expensive, costly

take *n.* 竹 bamboo

take *n.* 丈 length, height, stature

taki *n.* 滝 waterfall

taku *n.* 宅 home, house, residence, my husband

takusan no *adj.* 沢山の much, many

takushii *n.* タクシー taxi

tama *n.* 球 balls

tamago *n.* 卵 egg

tamashii *n.* 魂 soul, spirit

...no tame ni ...のために for, for the sake of, in the interest of

tambo *n.* たんぼ rice field

tana *n.* 棚 rack, shelf

tane *n.* 種 seed

tango *n.* 単語 word

tani *n.* 谷 valley, dale, vale

tanjōbi *n.* 誕生日 birthday

tanomu *vt.* 頼む ask, beg, ask a favor of, request, solicit
　tanomimasu (polite) 頼みます

tanoshii *adj.* 楽しい enjoyable, pleasant, delightful, cheerful

tansu *n.* 簞笥 chest of drawers, bureau, cabinet

tanzen *n.* たんぜん padded bathrobe

taoru *n.* タオル towel

tashika na *adj.* 確かな certain, sure, definite

tasukeru *vt.* 助ける help, aid, support
　tasukemasu (polite) 助けます

tatami *n.* 畳 mat, matting

tatoeba 例えば for instance, for example

tatsu *vi.* 立つ 1. leave, depart, set off 2. stand up, rise
　tachimasu (polite) 立ちます

tatta *adv.* たった only, merely, just

tawā *n.* タワー tower

tayori *n.* 便り news, correspondence, communication, letter

tazuneru *vt.* 尋ねる ask, inquire, look for, search
　tazunemasu (polite) 尋ねます

tebukuro *n.* 手袋 gloves

tēburu *n.* テーブル table

tegami *n.* 手紙 letter, note

teido *n.* 程度 degree, extent

teiki no *adj.* 定期の regular, fixed, periodical

tekitō na *adj.* 適当な suitable, proper, adequate, appropriate

tenisu kōto *n.* テニスコート tennis court

tenki *n.* 天気 weather
　o-tenki ga yoi お天気がよい the weather is fine

Tennō *n.* 天皇 Emperor

tensō *n.* 転送 forwarding, transmission (of mails)

tensō suru *vt.* 転送する forward

tenugui *n.* 手拭 hand towel

terebi *n.* テレビ television

tetsudau *vt.* 手伝う help, assist
　tetsudaimasu (polite) 手伝います

tetsudō *n.* 鉄道 railroad,

railway

...to *particle.* ...と and

tō *n.* 十 ten

tōka 十日 ten days, the tenth day

tōbun *adv.* 当分 for the present, for the time being, for some time, for a while

tochi *n.* 土地 land

tochū de 途中で on the way, en route, halfway, in the midst of

toden *n.* 都電 street car

todokeru *vt.* 届ける send, deliver, report

todokemasu (polite) 届けます

todoku *vi.* 届く arrive, reach, get to

todokimasu (polite) 届きます

tōhō 当方 our part, we

tōi *adj.* 遠い far

toiawaseru *vt.* 問い合わせる inquire, refer to

toiawasemasu (polite) 問い合わせます

tokei *n.* 時計 clock, watch

toki *n.* 時 time, hour, moment, occasion, opportunity, case, season

toko *n.* 床 bed

tokoya *n.* 床屋 barber

tokubetsu no *adj.* 特別の special

toku ni *adv.* 特に especially

tomaru *vi.* 泊まる stay, lodge

tomarimasu (polite) 泊まります

tomaru *vi.* 止まる stop, halt, pull up

tomarimasu (polite) 止まります

torakku *n.* トラック truck

torii *n.* 鳥居 front gate of

Shinto shrine

tōroku *n.* 登録 registration

tōroku suru 登録する register

tōroku shimasu (polite) 登録します

toru *vt.* 取る take, seize, catch, hold

torimasu (polite) 取ります

tōru *vi.* 通る pass, get through

tōrimasu (polite) 通ります

toshi *n.* 年 year

totemo *adv.* とても very, awfully

Tōyō *n.* 東洋 the East, the Orient

tsugi no *adj.* 次ぎの next, following, coming, ensuing, adjoining, second

tsuitachi *n.* 一日 the first day

tsuite *particle.* ...(に) ついて of, about, on, over, as to, concerning

tsukeru *vt.* 付ける attach, affix, fasten

tsukemasu (polite) 付けます

tsuki *n.* 月 month

hito-tsuki 一月 one month

tsukizuki 月々 every month

getsumatsu 月末 end of the month

tsuki *particle* ...(に)つき per, for

tsuku *vi.* 着く arrive, reach, get to

tsukimasu (polite) 着きます

tsuma *n.* 妻 wife, spouse,

okusama 奥様 your wife

kanai 家内 my wife

tsumari *adv.* つまり in a word, in short, that is, finally

tsume *n.* 爪 nail

tsuri *n.* 釣 fishing, angling

tsuru *vt.* 釣る fish

tsuri *n.* つり change (of money)
  o-tsuri (polite and commonly used) おつり

tsutomeru *vi.* 努 (勉) める be diligent, try hard, make every effort
  tsutomemasu (polite) 努 (勉) めます

tsutomesaki *n.* 勤め先 one's office, (one's place of) employment

tsutsumu *vt.* 包む wrap, cover, pack
  tsutsumimasu (polite) 包みます

tsuyoi *adj.* 強い strong, brave, firm

tsuzukeru *vt.* 続ける continue, carry on, go on
  tsuzukemasu (polite) 続けます

tsuzuri *n.* 綴り spelling (of words)

U

ude *n.* 腕 arm

udon *n.* うどん noodle

ue ni 上に on, above

ugokasu *vt.* 動かす move, remove, shift
  ugokashimasu (polite) 動かします

ugoku *vi.* 動く move, shift, shake
  ugokimasu (polite) 動きます

ukagau *vt.* 伺う (humble) call, visit, ask, question, inquire
  ukagaimasu (polite) 伺います

ukatsu na *adj.* 迂闊な careless, thoughtless, stupid

uketori *n.* 受取 receipt

uketsuke *n.* 受付 information desk, receptionist

umi *n.* 海 sea, ocean

unagi *n.* 鰻 eel

untenshu *n.* 運転手 driver

uo *n.* 魚 fish

ura *n.* 裏 reverse side, backside

ureru *vi.* 売れる sell, be in demand
  uremasu (polite) 売れます

ureshii *adj.* 嬉しい glad, joyful, delightful, happy

uru *vt.* 売る sell, offer (thing) for sale, deal in
  urimasu (polite) 売ります

ushiro *n.* 後 behind, rear

uso *n.* 嘘 lie, falsehood, fib, untruth
  uso o tsuku 嘘をつく lie

uta *n.* 歌 song

utagau *vt.* 疑う doubt, distrust, suspect
  utagaimasu (polite) 疑います

utau *vt.* 歌う sing, chant, recite, hum
  utaimasu (polite) 歌います

utsukushii *adj.* 美しい pretty, beautiful, fair, picturesque, good looking

uttōshii *adj.* うっとうしい gloomy, dismal, depressing, unpleasant, dull, heavy

uwagi *n.* 上着 jacket

W

waishatsu *n.* ワイシャツ shirt

wakai *adj.* 若い young, youthful

wakaru *vt.* 分る understand, comprehend
  wakarimasu (polite) 分ります

wake *n.* 訳 reason, meaning, cause

wakeru *vt.* 分ける divide, part, separate
  wakemasu (polite) 分けます

waki *n.* 脇 side

warau *vt.* 笑う laugh

waraimasu (polite) 笑います

waribiki *n.* 割引 discount, rebate, reduction

waribiki suru *vt.* 割引する give a discount, reduce

warui *adj.* 悪い bad, evil, ill, wrong

wasureru *vt.* 忘れる forget, leave behind

  wasuremasu (polite) 忘れます

watakushi, watashi *pron.* 私 I, me

  watakushi no, watashi no 私 の my, mine

wazato *adv.* わざと purposely, on purpose, intentionally

Y

...ya *conj.* ...や and

yaburu *vt.* 破る tear, rip, rend, violate, infringe, destroy, crush

  yaburimasu (polite) 破ります

yahari *adv.* やはり also, too, as well, likewise, either

yakamashii *adj.* 喧しい noisy, clamorous

yakeru *vi.* 焼ける burn

  yakemasu (polite) 焼けます

yakitsuke *n.* 焼付 printing (of a picture)

yaku *vt.* 焼く burn

  yakimasu (polite) 焼きます

yaku *adv.* 約 approximately, about, nearly, around

yakunin *n.* 役人 government official, public servant

yakusoku *n.* 約束 promise, engagement, appointment

yakusoku suru *vt.* 約束する promise, make an engagement

yakyū *n.* 野球 baseball

yama 山 mountain

yameru *vt.* 止める stop, give up, abandon

  yamemasu (polite) 止めます

yamu *vi.* 止む stop, cease

  yamimasu (polite) 止みます

yane *n.* 屋根 roof

yani *n.* やに resin

yasai *n.* 野菜 vegetables

yasashii *adj.* 優しい gentle, tender, kind, kindhearted

yasashii *adj.* 易しい easy, plain, simple

yasui *adj.* 安い cheap, inexpensive, low-priced

yasumu *vi.* 休む rest, be absent

  yasumimasu (polite) 休みます

yattsu *n.* 八つ eight

  yōka 八日 eight days, the eighth day

yawarakai *adj.* 柔かい soft, gentle, mild, tender

yobu *vt.* 呼ぶ call

  yobimasu (polite) 呼びます

yogoreru *vi.* 汚れる become dirty

  yogoremasu (polite) 汚れます

yogoreta *adj.* 汚れた dirty, soiled, stained

yoi *adj.* よい fine, good, nice

yōji *n.* 用事 business, errand

yōjin *n.* 用心 care, caution, prudence, circumspection

yōjinbukai *adj.* 用心深い careful, cautious, prudent, watchful

yōkoso *int.* ようこそ welcome!

yoku *adv.* よく well, nicely, splendidly, fully, enough, thoroughly

yomu *vt.* 読む read

  yomimasu (polite) 読みます

yon *n.* 四 four

yonjū-shi 四十四 forty-four

yoreba *particle* ...(に)よれば according to

yorokonde *adv.* 喜んで gladly, joyfully, willingly, with pleasure

yoron *n.* 世論 public opinion, popular voice, public sentiment

yoroshii *adj.* よろしい good, appropriate, well, all right

yoroshiku *adv.* よろしく one's regards, one's best wishes
　Dōzo yoroshiku どうぞよろ
　しく How do you do?

yoru *n.* 夜 night

yōsu *n.* 様子 condition, state, circumstance, phase, aspect,

yotei *n.* 予定 expectation, anticipation, schedule, plan

yottsu *n.* 四 four
　yoji 四時 four o'clock
　yokka 四日 four days, the fourth day

yowai *adj.* 弱い weak, frail, feeble

yoyaku *n.* 予約 reservation, booking
　yoyaku suru *vt.* 予約する reserve

yūbe 昨夜 last night

yūbin *n.* 郵便 mail
　yūbin-ya 郵便屋 mailman, postman
　yūbinkyoku 郵便局 post office
　yūbinryōkin 郵便料金 postage

yubiwa *n.* 指輪 ring

yūbō na *adj.* 有望な promising

yūdachi *n.* 夕立 (rain) shower

yūgata *n.* 夕方 evening

yūhan *n.* 夕飯 dinner, supper

yuka *n.* 床 floor

yukai na *adj.* 愉快な pleasant, delightful, joyful, jolly, happy, cheerful

yuki *n.* 雪 snow

yukkuri *adv.* ゆっくり slowly

yūkō na *adj.* 有効な valid, effective

yume *n.* 夢 dream, vision, illusion

yunyū *n.* 輸入 import, importation

yunyū suru *vt.* 輸入する import

yurusu *vt.* 許す 1. allow, permit, grant, authorize 2. forgive, excuse
　yurushimasu (polite) 許します

yūshoku *n.* 夕食 dinner, supper

yushutsu *n.* 輸出 export, exportation
　yushutsu suru *vt.* 輸出する export

yūutsu na *adj.* 憂鬱な melancholy, cheerless, gloomy, dejected, depressed, blue

yūyake *n.* 夕焼け evening glow, afterglow, sunset colors

Z

zairyō *n.* 材料 material, matter, stuff

zaisan *n.* 財産 fortune, means, property

zannen na *adj.* 残念な regrettable, disappointing
　zannen desu *vi.* 残念です too bad, be disappointed, feel sorry

zashiki *n.* 座敷 drawing room

zasshi *n.* 雑誌 magazine, journal, periodical

zeikan *n.* 税関 customs

zeikin *n.* 税金 tax, duty

zeitaku *n.* 贅沢 luxury
　zeitakuhin 贅沢品 an article of luxury

zeitaku na *adj.* luxurious

zembu *n.* 全部 all, entire, whole

zonjiru *vt.* 存じる (*humble form of*) know, be aware of, be acquainted with

zōri *n.* 草履 sandals for kimono

zubon *n.* ズボン trousers

...zutsu *suf.* ...ずつ each, apiece

zutto *adv.* ずっと 1. straight 2. by far, long before 3. all the time, throughout

zūzūshii *adj.* 図々しい audacious, impudent

ENGLISH-JAPANESE DICTIONARY

In this dictionary the English entry is followed by the Japanese transliteration which, in turn, is followed by the same word in Japanese script. Adjectives of Class II are given with the particle *na*. Verbs are given in the present form. Where a given entry is capable of appearing in a variety of contexts, the most important of these are cited.

A

abandon *vt.* suteru (leave completely) 捨てる
yameru (give up) 止める

ability *n.* nōryoku 能力

able *adj.* dekiru *v.i.* 出来る

aboard *prep.* ...ni notte... に乗って

about *prep.* no mawari ni (around) のまわりに ...goro (time) ...ごろ ...ni tsuite (concerning) について *adv.* oyoso およそ yaku 約 (almost) atari ni (somewhere around) あたりに

above *prep.* ...no ue ni *adv. phr.* の上に ...ijō no (over) 以上の *adv.* ue ni *adv. ph.* 上に

abroad *adv.* gaikoku e 外国へ

absent *adj.* rusu ni suru (from home) 留守にする yasumu (from school, work etc.) 休む

absolutely *adv.* hontō ni 本当に

academic *adj.* gakumon no 学問の

accept *vt.* ukeru 受ける itadaku 頂く (polite) chōdai suru 頂戴する (polite)

accident *n.* jiko 事故

accommodations *n.* (place to stay) tomaru tokoro 泊まる所

accompany *vt.* ...to issho ni iku と一緒に行く ...no otomo o suru (humble) のお供をする

accomplish *vt.* shitogeru (carry out)仕遂げる shitogeru (finish) 仕上げる

accordance *n.* itchi 一致 **in accordance with** ...ni shitagatte ...に従って ...no tōri ni ...の通りに

according to *adv.* ...ni yoru to によると ...ni yore ba ...によれば ...ni yotte ...によって

account *n.* kanjyō 勘定

accurate *adj.* seikaku na 正確な seimitsu na 精密な

accuse *v.t.* togameru とがめる hinansuru 非難する

ache *vi.* itamu 痛む uzuku うずく

achieve *v.t.* shitogeru 仕遂げる

acknowledge *v.t.* mitomeru 認める shōnin suru 承認する

acquaintance *n.* shiriai 知合 najimi 馴染

across *prep.* ...no mukō ni ...の向うに ...o yoko gitte ...を横切って

act *vt.* suru (do) する enjiru (perform) 演じる *vi.* furumau (behave) 振舞う

action *n.* okonai 行い kōdō 行動 kōi 行為 dōsa 動作

active *adj.* koppatsu na 活発な

actually *adv.* hontō ni 本当に

acute *adj.* hageshii 烈しい

add *vt.*, *vi.* kuwaeru 加える tsuika suru 追加する

address *n.* jyūsho 住所 atena (on a letter) 宛名

adequate *adj.* tekitō na 適当な

adjoining *adj.* tonari no 隣の

adjust *vt.* awasu (fit) 合わす totonoeru(put in order)整える chōsetsusuru (fix) 調節する

administration *n.* (of office, factory, etc.) kanri, 管理, keiei 経営 (of politics) seiji 政治 gyosei 行政

admit *vt.* ireru (let in) 入れる mitomeru (acknowledge) 認める shōnin suru 承認する

advance *vt.* susumeru 進める *vi.* susumu 進む *n.* zenshin (move forward) 前進 shimpo 進歩 hattatsu (progress) 発達 **in advance** mae motte 前以て

advertisement *n.* kōkoku 広告

advice *n.* chūkoku 忠告

affair *n.* koto 事

affection *n.* aijō 愛情

afford *vt.* ...suru yoyū ga aru (expense) ...する余裕がある *vi.* ...dekiru ...出来る

after *prep.* no ato de の後で *conj.* no nochi ni の後に

afternoon *n.* gogo 午後 **good afternoon** kon-nichi wa 今日は

again *adv.* mō ichido もう一度

against *prep.* ...ni taishite ...に対して ...ni hantai shite ...に反対して ...ni mukkatte ...に向かって

age *n.* toshi 年

agency *n.* kikan 機関

ago *adj.* *adv.* mae ni 前に

agree *vt.* sanseisuru (consent) 賛成する dōisuru 同意する itchisuru (come to one) 一致する

agreement *n.* sansei (consent) 賛成 dōi 同意 itchi (concord) 一致

agriculture *n.* nōgyō 農業

ahead *adv.* saki ni 先に mae ni 前に

aid *vt.* tasukeru 助ける tetsudau (to assist) 手伝う

aim at *vi.* nerau 狙う *vt.* mezasu 目指す

air *n.* kūki 空気

airline kōkūgaisha 航空会社

air mail kōkū yūbin 航空郵便

airport hikōjyō 飛行場

airplane hikōki 飛行機

aisle *n.* tsūro 通路

alarm *vt.* odorokasu 驚かす

alarm clock mezamashi-dokei めざまし時計

be alarmed odoroku 驚く

a la carte *phr.* ippin ryori *n.* 一品料理

alike *adj.* onaji 同じ

all *n.* zenbu 全部 minna, mina 皆 *adj.* arayuru あらゆる

allow *vt.* yurusu 許す

almost *adv.* hotondo ほとんど o kata おおかた

alone *adv.* hitori de 独りで

along *prep.* ...ni sotte ...にそって

already *adv.* sude ni すでに mo もう

also *adv.* mo も mo mata もまた yahari やはり

alternately *adv.* kawara gawaru かわるがわる kōgo ni 交互に

although *conj.* ...keredomo ...けれども ...to wa ie ...とはいえ

altogether *adv.* minna de 皆で

issho ni 一緒に

always *adv.* itsumo いつも

a. m. *n.* gozen 午前

ambiguous *adj.* aimai na あいまいな bakuzen to shita 漠然とした

ambulance *n.* kyūkyūsha 救急車

America *n.* Amerika アメリカ Beikoku 米国

American *adj.* Amerika no アメリカの Beikoku no 米国の *n.* Amerikajin アメリカ人 Beikokujin 米国人

amend *vt.* teisei suru 訂正する

among *prep.* ...no naka ni ...の中に ...no aida ni ...の間に

amount to *vi.* ...ni naru ...になる

ample *adj.* jūbun na 充分な

amusement *n.* asobi 遊び goraku 娯楽

amusing *adj.* omoshiroi おもしろい okashii (funny) おかしい

and *conj.* ...to ...と ...ya や sōshite そうして

animal *n.* dōbutsu 動物

announce *vt.* shiraseru 知らせる happyō suru (publicly) 発表する

announcement *n.* tsūchi 通知

annoying *adj.* urusai うるさい

another *adj.* mō hitotsu no もう一つの betsu no 別の

answer *n.* kotae 答 henji 返事 kaito 解答 *vt.* kotaeru 答える henji suru 返事する

anticipate *vt.* yosō suru (foresee) 予想する kitai suru (expect) 期待する

anxious *adj.* shimpai na 心配な kigakari na 気がかりな

anybody *pron.* dare ka (interrogative) 誰か dare demo (affir-

mative) 誰でも dare mo (negative) 誰も

anything *pron.* nani ka (interrogative) 何か nan demo (affirmative) 何でも nani mo (negative) 何も

any time *adv.* itsu de mo いつでも

anywhere *adv.* doko ka (interrogative) どこか doko demo (affirmative) どこでも doko mo (negative) どこも

apiece *adv.* ...zutsu ...ずつ

apologize *vt.* wabiru 詫びる ayamaru 謝る

apparatus *n.* sōchi 装置 shikake 仕掛け

apparently *adv.* akiraka ni 明らかに

appear *vi.* mieru 見える

appetite *n.* shokuyoku 食欲

apple *n.* ringo りんご

apple pie appuru pai アップルパイ

application *n.* mōshikomi 申し込み

appointment *n.* (engagement) yakusoku 約束

appreciate *vt.* arigataku omou 有難く思う kansha suru 感謝する

approach *vi.* chikazuku 近づく

appropriate *adj.* (proper) tekitō na 適当な

approve *vt.* (recognize) sansei suru 賛成する shōnin suru 承認する

approximately *adv.* daitai 大体 oyoso 凡そ

April *n.* Shi-gatsu 四月

architecture *n.* kenchiku 建築

area *n.* chiiki (region) 地域 han-i (scope) 範囲 menseki (space)

面積

arm *n.* ude 腕

around *prep.* …no mawari ni …のまわりに *adv.* oyoso およそ yaku (about) 約

arrangement *n.* haichi 配置 toriawase 取合せ

arrangements *n.* shitaku (preparation) 支度 jumbi 準備

arrive *vi.* tsuku 着く

art *n.* bijutsu (fine art) 美術 geijutsu 芸術

art gallery bijutsukan 美術館

as *prep.* …to shite wa (in the function of) …としては *conj.* …shinagara (while) …しながら …no yō ni (like) …のように

ascertain *vt.* tashikameru 確かめる

ashes *n.* hai 灰

ash tray *n.* haizara 灰皿

ask *vt.* (question) kiku 聞く tazuneru 尋ねる (a favor) tanomu 頼む

assist *vt.* tetsudau 手伝う tasukeru 助ける

association *n.* kyōkai 協会

assure *vt.* hoshō suru (insure) 保証する kakushin saseru (convince) 確信させる

at *prep.* …ni に …de で

atmosphere *n.* kūki (air) 空気 fun-iki (circumstances) 雰囲気

attach *vt.* tsukeru 付ける

attention *n.* chūi 注意

attractive *adj.* aikyō no aru 愛嬌のある

August *n.* Hachi-gatsu 八月

aunt *n.* oba (san) 伯母 (elder than parent) 叔母 (younger than parent)

automobile *n.* jidōsha 自動車

autumn *n.* aki 秋

average *n.* heikin 平均 *adj.* heikin no 平均の futsū no 普通の

avoid *vt.* sakeru 避ける

awkward *adj.* guai ga warui (embarrassing) 工合が悪い fuben na (unhandy) 不便な

B

baby *n.* akachan 赤ちゃん akambo あかんぼ, 赤坊

back *n.* (behind) ushiro 後 (of body) senaka 背中

bad *adj.* warui 悪い dame na 駄目な (unskillful) heta na 下手な

bag *n.* fukuro 袋 kaban かばん

baggage *n.* nimotsu 荷物

ball *n.* tama 球

bamboo *n.* take 竹

bamboo work takezaiku 竹細工

bank *n.* ginkō 銀行

banquet *n.* enkai 宴会

barber *n.* tokoya 床屋

baseball *n.* yakyū 野球

basement *n.* chika 地下

basket *n.* kago 籠

basketball *n.* basuketto bōru バスケットボール

bath *n.* furo 風呂

bathing suit *n.* mizugi 水着

bean *n.* mame 豆

beautiful *adj.* kirei na 綺麗な utukushii 美しい mimeyoshi みめよし

because *conj.* …kara …から …node …ので …no tame のため

become *vi.* naru なる (suits) niau 似合う

bed *n*. shindai 寝台 toko 床

beefsteak *n*. bifuteki ビフテキ

beer *n*. biiru ビール

before *prep*. ...no mae ni の前に

begin *vt*. hajimeru 始める *vi*. 始まる

behavior *n*. gyōgi 行儀 okonai 行い

behind *prep*. ...no ushiro ni... の後に

believe *vt*. shinjiru 信じる omou (think) 思う *vi*. kangaeru 考える

bell *n*. beru ベル

below *prep*. ...no shita ni ...の下に

beside *prep*. ...no soba ni ...のそばに

besides *adv*. sono ue ni その上に sarani さらに

best *adj*. ichiban ii 一番いい ichiban yoi 一番良い goku ii 極くいい goku yoi 極く良い

better *adj*. motto ii もっといい motto yoi もっと良い ...yori ii よりいい ...yori yoi より良い

between *prep*. ...no aida ni...の間に

beyond *prep*. ...no mukō ni ...の向うに

Bible *n*. seisho 聖書

bicycle *n*. jitensha 自転車

big *adj*. ōkii 大きい

bill *n*. kanjō 勘定

bind *vt*. shibaru しばる yuwaeru ゆわえる

bird *n*. tori 鳥

birthday *n*. tanjōbi 誕生日

bit *n*. sukoshi (small portion) 少し

bitter *adj*. nigai 苦い

black *adj*. kuroi 黒い *n*. kuro 黒

blanket *n*. mōfu 毛布

blood *n*. chi 血

bloom *vi*. saku 咲く

blotter *n*. suitorigami 吸取紙

blow *vi*. fuku 吹く

blue *adj*. aoi 青い *n*. ao 青

boat *n*. fune 舟

bone *n*. hone 骨

book *n*. hon 本

bookcase hon-bako 本箱

bookshelf hon-dana 本棚

bookshop hon-ya 本屋

boot *n*. nagagutsu 長靴

borrow *vt*. kariru 借りる

both *adv*. ryōhō tomo 両方とも dochira mo どちらも

bother *n*. mendō 面倒 meiwaku 迷惑 mendō o kakeru 面倒をかける meiwaku o kakeru 迷惑をかける

bottle *n*. bin びん
one bottle hito bin 一びん

bottle opener sennuki 栓抜き

bottom *n*. soko 底

bouquet *n*. hanataba 花束

bow *n*. ojigi お辞儀 *vi*. ojigi o suru お辞儀をする

bowl *n*. chawan 茶碗
one bowl ippai 一杯

box *n*. hako 箱

boy *n*. otoko no ko 男の子 (polite) botchan 坊ちゃん musuko (son) 息子

bracelet *n*. udewa 腕輪

brand *n*. shirushi 印 shōhyō (trade mark) 商標

brazier *n*. hibachi 火鉢

bread *n*. pan パン

break vi. kowareru 毀れる vt. kowasu 毀す

breakfast n. asahan 朝飯 chō-shoku 朝食

bridge n. hashi 橋

brief adj. mijikai (short) 短い kantan na (concise) 簡単な adv. mijikaku 短く kantan ni 簡単に

briefcase n. kaban かばん

bright adj. akarui 明るい rikō-na (intelligent) りこうな

bring vt. (a thing) motte kuru 持って来る (a person) tsurete kuru 連れて来る

broad adj. hiroi 広い

broadcast vt. vi. hōsō suru (radio) 放送する

broadcasting station hōsōkyo-ku 放送局

brothers n. kyōdai 兄弟

brown adj. chairo no 茶色の n. chairo 茶色

Buddhism n. Bukkyō 仏教

Buddhist temple (o-)tera (お)寺

budget n. yosan 予算

build vt. tateru 建てる

bureau n. kyoku (department) 局 tansu (chest) たんす

burglar n. dorobō 泥棒

burn vi. yakeru 焼ける vt. yaku 焼く moyasu 燃やす

bus n. basu バス

business n. (enterprise) jitsugyō 実業 (commerce) shōgyō 商業 (errand) yōji 用事

businessman jitsugyōka 実業家

busy adj. isogashii 忙しい

but conj. ...ga ...が keredomo けれども shikashi しかし

button n. botan ボタン vt. botan o kakeru ボタンをかける

buy vt. kau ·買う

by prep. ...no soba ni ...のそばに (not later than) ...made ni 迄に

by means of adv. ...de (particle) ...で

C

cable n. dempō 電報

cake n. (o-)kashi (お)菓子

cabin n. kabin キャビン

calendar n. koyomi 暦

call vt. yobu 呼ぶ

calling card meishi 名刺

camera n. shashin-ki 写真機 kamera カメラ

can n. kan 缶

canned goods kanzume 缶詰

can opener kankiri 缶切り

can aux. v. dekiru 出来る

cannot aux. v. dekinai 出来ない

cancel vt. torikesu 取消す

candle n. rōsoku ろうそく

candy n. (o-)kashi (お)菓子

candy store kashiya 菓子屋

cap n. bōshi 帽子

capital n. (money) shihon 資本 shikin 資金 (city) shufu 首府

capitalism n. shihonshugi 資本主義

car n. kuruma 車

care n. yōjin 用心 chūi 注意 vt. yōjin suru 用心する chūi suru 注意する

careful adj. ki o tsukeru (cautious) 気をつける chūi-bukai (watchful) 注意深い yō-jinbukai 用心深い

careless adj. fuchūi na 不注意 na ukatsu na 迂闊な

carry vt. motte iku 持って行く hakobu 運ぶ

cartoon n. manga 漫画

carving *n.* chōkoku 彫刻 hori-mono 彫物

case *n.* (circumstance) baai 場合 (box) hako 箱

cash *n.* genkin 現金 *vt.* genkin ni kaeru 現金に変える genkin ni suru 現金にする

    cash a large bill komakaku suru 細かくする kuzusu くずす

casual *adj.* nanige nai 何げない

cat *n.* neko 猫

catalog *n.* katarogu カタログ

catch *vt.* toru 取る tsukamu 掴む (train) maniau 間に合う

cause *n.* (of an effect) gen-in 原因 (reason) wake わけ riyū 理由 (purpose) tame 為
    vt. okosu 起す

cautious *adj.* yōjinbukai 用心深い

cease *vi.* yameru 止める

center *n.* mannaka 真中 chū-shin 中心

certain *adj.* tashikana 確かな

chair *n.* isu 椅子

chance *n.* gūzen 偶然
    by chance *adv.* gūzen ni 偶然に

change *vi.* kawaru 変わる *vt.* kaeru 変える (train) norikaeru 乗り変える *n.* henka 変化 komakai o-kane (small money) 細かいお金 (o-)tsuri (money returned) おつり

character *n.* seikaku (person) 性格 tokuchō (feature) 特徴 seishitsu (thing) 性質

charge *n.* ryōkin (money) 料金

chauffeur *n.* untenshu 運転手

cheap *adj.* yasui 安い

cheat *vt.* damasu だます goma-kasu ごまかす
    be cheated damasareru だま

される gomakasareru ごまかされる

check *n.* kogitte (money) 小切手 chikki (baggage) チッキ *vt.* shiraberu (investigate) 調べる azukeru (to leave in temporary custody) 預ける chikki de o-kuru (to send under the privilege of a ticket) チッキで送る

cherry *n.* sakura 桜

cherry blossoms sakura no hana 桜の花

chest *n.* mune 胸

child *n.* ko 子 kodomo 子供
    your child (polite) o-kosan お子さん
    children kodomo-tachi *pl.* 子供達

chilly *adv.* samui (weather) 寒い tsumetai (temperature) 冷たい

chimney *n.* entotsu 煙突

China *n.* Chūgoku 中国

Chinese *adj.* Chūgoku no 中国の *n.* Chūgokujin (people) 中国人 Chūgokugo (language) 中国語

Chinese character (writing) *n.* kanji 漢字

choose *vt.* erabu 選ぶ

chopsticks *n.* (o-)hashi (お)箸

Christianity *n.* Kiristo-kyō キリスト教

chrysanthemum *n.* kiku 菊

church *n.* kyōkai 教会

cigar *n.* hamaki 葉巻

cigarette *n.* tabako タバコ

cigarette case tabako-ire タバコ入れ

cigarette holder paipu パイプ

circle *n.* maru 丸 en 円

circulate *vi.* mawaru 廻る *vt.* mawasu 廻す

circumstance n. jijō 事情

city n. machi 街 shi 市

clean adj. kirei na きれいな vt. kirei ni suru きれいにする sōji suru 掃除する

clear adj. akarui (bright) 明るい sunda (lucid) 澄んだ hareta (opp. to dark) 晴れた meiryō na (distinct) 明瞭な vt. kiyoku suru (make clean) 清くする vi. hareru (become clear) 晴れる

clearly adv. hakkiri to はっきりと

clerk n. jimu-in 事務員 (in shop) ten-in 店員

clever adj. rikō na 利口な

cliff n. gake 崖

climate n. kikō 気候

climb vt. noboru のぼる

clock n. tokei 時計

close vt. shimeru 閉める tojiru 閉じる vi. shimaru 閉まる

cloudy adj. kumori (gachi) 曇り（がち）

coast n. kaigan 海岸

coat n. kōto コート

coffee n. kōhii コーヒー

coffee cup kohii-jawan コーヒー茶碗

coffee house kōhii-ten コーヒー店

cold adj. samui (weather) 寒い tsumetai (temperature) 冷い n. kaze 風邪

　catch cold kaze o hiku 風邪をひく

collapse vi. tsubureru (building) つぶれる taoreru (person) 倒れる

collar n. eri えり

collect vi. atsumaru 集まる vt. atsumeru 集める

college n. daigaku 大学

collision n. shōtotsu 衝突

color n. iro 色

comb n. kushi 櫛 vt. kami o tokasu (hair) 髪をとかす

combination ι. kumiawase 組合せ

combine vt. awaseru 合せる kumiawaseru 組合せる

come vi. kuru 来る irassharu (polite) いらっしゃる mairu (humble) 参る

comedy n. kigeki 喜劇

comfortable adj. raku na 楽な kimochi no yoi 気持のよい

comics n. manga 漫画

commerce n. shōgyō 商業

commodity n. shinamono 品物 shōhin 商品

commodity price bukka 物価

common adj. futsū no 普通の

common sense jōshiki 常識

Communism n. kyōsanshugi 共産主義

company n. kaisha (firm) 会社 kōsai (friendship) 交際

compare vt. kuraberu 比べる hikaku suru 比較する

compete vi. kisou 競う kyōsō suru 競争する

complain vi. fuhei o iu 不平を云う

complaint n. fuhei 不平

complete adj. kanzen na 完全な vt. shiageru (finish) 仕上げる kansei suru (make perfect) 完成する

completely adv. kanzen ni 完全に mattaku 全く sukkari すっかり

completion n. dekiagari 出来上がり

complicated adj. fukuzatsu na

複雑な komi-itta 込み入つた
compliment n. o-seji お世辞
compromise n. dakyō 妥協 vi. dakyō suru 妥協する
concerning prep. ....ni tsuite ...について
concert n. ongakukai 音楽会
conclusion n. ketsuron 結論
condition n. jōtai 状態 yōsu 様子 (stipulation) jōken 条件
confidence n. shin-yō 信用
confident adj. kataku shinjite 固く信じて shin-yō shite 信用して
confirm vt. tashikameru 確かめる
confused adj. menkuratta 面くらった konran shita 混乱した mecha mecha na 目茶目茶な
congratulations! n. Omedeto! おめでとう Omedeto go-zaimasu! おめでとうございます
connect vi. tsunagaru つながる vt. tsunagu つなぐ
be connected with kankei ga aru 関係がある
conscience n. ryōshin 良心
consent vi. sansei suru 賛成する shōchi suru 承知する
consider vt. kangaeru 考える
constitution n. kempō 憲法
consulate n. ryōji-kan 領事館
consult vi. sōdan suru 相談する
contact n. renraku 連絡 sessho-ku 接触 vt. renraku suru 連絡する
contain vt. fukumu 含む ...ga haitte iru vi. が入っている
continue vt. tsuzukeru 続ける
contract n. keiyaku 契約
contradiction n. mujun 予盾

contrary adj. hantai no 反対の
on the contrary kaette かえって
contrary to ...ni hanshite...に反して
contribution n. kifu (gift) 寄附 shusshi (investment) 出資
control vt. torishimaru 取締る
convenience n. benri 便利
convenient adj. benri na 便利な
cooking n. ryōri 料理
cool adj. suzushii 涼しい reisei na (unexcited) 冷静な reitan na (lacking zeal) 冷淡な
copy n. utsushi 写し vt. utsusu 写す
corner n. (outside) kado 角 (inside) sumi すみ
correct adj. tadashii 正しい vt. naosu 直す tadasu 正す teisei suru 訂正する
corridor n. rōka 廊下
cosmetics n. keshōhin 化粧品
cost n. nedan 値段 vi. kakaru かかる
cough n. seki 咳 vi. seki o suru 咳をする
count vt. kazoeru 数える
counter n. kauntā カウンター
country n. (nation) kuni 国 (countryside) inaka 田舎
course n. kōsu コース
courteous adj. reigi tadashii 礼儀正しい ingin na いんぎんな
cousin n. itoko いとこ
cover vt. ōu 被う tsutsumu 包む
crab n. kani かに
crazy adj. ki ga chigatta (insane) 気がちがつた muchū no (madly eager) 夢中の
be crazy for... ...ni muchū desu ...に夢中です

credit *n.* shin-yō 信用
crisis *n.* kiki 危機
criticism *n.* hihyō 批評 hihan 批判
cross (**over**) *vt.* kosu 越す
crossing *n.* kōsaten 交叉点 fumikiri (railroad) ふみきり
crowded *adj.* konde iru こんでいる
crush *vi.* tsubureru つぶれる *vt.* tsubusu つぶす
culture *n.* bunka (civilization) 文化 kyōyō (refinement) 教養
cup *n.* chawan 茶碗
　one cup ippai 一杯
　two cups nihai 二杯
cure *vt.* naosu なおす
curious *adj.* monozuki na 物好きな
curry *n.* karē カレー
curry rice karē raisu カレーライス
custom *n.* shūkan 習慣
customs *n.* zeikan 税関
cut *vi.* kireru 切れる *vt.* kiru 切る
cute *adj.* kawaii 可愛い
cutlet (**pork**) *n.* katsuretsu カツレツ

D

danger *n.* kiken 危険
dangerous *adj.* abunai 危い
dark *adj.* kurai 暗い
date *n.* (of month) hizuke 日付け (engagement) yakusoku 約束
daughter *n.* musume 娘
　your daughter (polite) o-jōsan お嬢さん
dawn *n.* yoake 夜明け
day *n.* hi 日 hiruma 昼間
day after tomorrow asatte 明

後日
day before yesterday ototoi 一昨日
deadline *n.* kigen 期限
debt *n.* shakkin 借金
December *n.* Jūni-gatsu 十二月
decide *vt.* kimeru 決める
deck *n.* dekki デッキ
deep *adj.* fukai 深い
degree *n.* teido 程度
delay *vi.* okureru 遅れる
delicious *adj.* oishii おいしい
delightful *adj.* ureshii (happy) うれしい tanoshii (pleasant) 楽しい omoshiroi (amusing) 面白い
deliver *vt.* todokeru 届ける
democracy *n.* minshushugi 民主主義 demokurashii デモクラシー
demonstration *n.* demonsutorēshon デモンストレーション
dentist *n.* haisha 歯医者
deny *vt.* kobamu 拒む uchikesu 打消す
depart *vi.* deru 出る shuppatsu suru 出発する
department (**store**) *n.* depāto デパート
departure *n.* shuppatsu 出発
description *n.* setsumei 説明
desire *vt.* nozomu 望む hoshii desu 欲しいです *n.* nozomi 望み
desk *n.* tsukue 机
dessert *n.* dezāto デザート
destroy *vt.* kowasu 毀す horobosu (annihilate) 滅す
detailed *adj.* kuwashii 詳しい shōsai na 詳細な
determine *vt.* kimeru 決める *vi.* kesshin suru (resolve) 決心する
dialect *n.* namari 訛り hōgen

方言

diary *n.* nikki 日記

dictionary *n.* jibiki 字引

differ *vi.* chigau 違う

different *adj.* chigatta 違つた betsu no 別の

difficult *adj.* muzukashii むずかしい

dining car shokudō sha 食堂車

dining room shokudō 食堂

dinner *n.* yūshoku 夕食 yūhan 夕飯

direction *n.* hōkō 方向

directly *adv.* (straight ahead) massugu ni 真直に (immediately) chokusetsu ni 直接に

dirty *adj.* kitanai きたない

discount *n.* waribiki 割引

disease *n.* byōki 病気

dish *n.* sara 皿

dislike *vt.* kirau 嫌う

distant *adj.* tōi 遠い

distinctly *adv.* hakkiri to はっきりと

divide *vi.* wakareru 分れる *vt.* wakeru 分ける

do *vt.* suru する itasu (humble) いたす
nasaru (polite) なさる

doctor *n.* isha 医者

dog *n.* inu 犬

doll *n.* ningyō 人形

dollar *n.* doru ドル

door *n.* doa ドア to 戸

double *adj.* nibai no 二倍の nijū no (twofold) 二重の *vt.* nibai ni suru 二倍にする *vi.* nibai ni naru 二倍になる

doubt *n.* utagai 疑 gimon 疑問 *vt.* utagau 疑う

down *prep.* shita e 下へ

dozen *n.* dāsu ダース

dream *n.* yume 夢 *vi.* yume o miru 夢をみる

dressing (for food) *n.* chōmiryō 調味料

drink *vt.* nomu 飲む *n.* nomimono 飲みもの

driver *n.* untenshu 運転手

drop *vi.* ochiru 落ちる *vt.* otosu 落す

drugstore *n.* kusuriya 薬屋

dry *vi.* kawaku 乾く *vt.* kawakasu 乾かす *adj.* kawaita 乾いた

dull *adj.* (person, thing) nibui 鈍い (color, sound) saenai さえない (day, story) taikutsu na 退屈な

during *prep.* ...no aida ...の間

dust *n.* hokori ほこり chiri 塵 *vt.* hokori o harau ほこりを払う

duty *n.* (obligation) gimu 義務 tsutome 務め sekinin 責任 (tax) zei 税
customs duties kanzei 関税
export (**import**) **duties** yushutsu (yunyū) zei 輸出(輸入)税

E

each *adv.* ...zutsu ...ずつ

each other o-tagai ni お互に

ear *n.* mimi 耳

early *adj.* hayai 早い *adv.* hayaku 早く

earnest *adj.* majime na まじめな

earthquake *n.* jishin 地震

ease *n.* anshin 安心 kiraku 気楽
feel easy anshin suru 安心する

east *n*. higashi 東
easy *adj*. yasashii やさしい
eat *vt*. taberu 食べる itadaku (humble) 頂く meshiagaru (polite) 召し上がる
economy *n*. keizai 経済
edge *n*. fuchi 縁 hashi 端 ·(of knife) ha 刃
education *n*. kyōiku 教育
eel *n*. unagi うなぎ
effect *n*. kikime ききめ kōka 効果
egg *n*. tamago 卵
eight *n*. hachi 八 yattsu 八つ
eighteen jūhachi 十八
eighth day yōka 八日
eighty hachi-jū 八十
either one dochira demo どちらでも
electric *adj*. denki no 電気の
electric blanket denki mōfu 電気毛布
electric bulb denkyū 電球
electric clock denkidokei 電気時計
electricity *n*. denki 電気
electric light dentō 電燈
elevator *n*. erebētā エレベーター
embassy *n*. taishikan 大使館
emergency *n*. kyūba 急場 hijō no baai 非常の場合
emergency exit hijō-guchi 非常口
in case of emergency hijō no baai niwa 非常の場合には
Emperor *n*. tennō 天皇・
enclose *vt*. dōfū suru 同封する
end *n*. owari 終り *vi*. owaru 終る
energy *n*. enerugii エネルギー
engagement *n*. yakusoku (date) 約束 kon-yaku (betrothal) 婚約

England *n*. Eikoku 英国 Igirisu イギリス
English *adj*. Eikoku no 英国の *n*. Eikokujin (people) 英国人 Eigo (language) 英語
enjoy *vt*. tanoshimu 楽しむ
enough *adj*. jūbun na 充分な *adv*. jūbun ni 充分に
enter *vi*. hairu 入る
entertain *vt*. motenasu もてなす
entirely *adv*. sukkari すっかり mattaku 全く zenzen 全然
entrance *n*. iriguchi 入口
envelope *n*. fūtō 封筒
equivalent *adj*. ...ni hitoshii ...に等しい
error *n*. machigai 間違い
escalator *n*. esukarētā エスカレーター
especially *adj*. toku ni 特に koto ni 殊に
essential *adj*. hitsuyō na 必要な
estimate *n*. mitsumori 見積り *vt*. mitsumoru 見積る
et cetera (etc.) ...nado...等
even *adv*. ...demo (*particle*) ...も
evening *n*. ban 晩 yūgata 夕方 **good evening** komban wa 今晩は
every *adj*. dono......mo どの......も minna 皆 arayuru (all possible) あらゆる mai········· (each) 毎·········
everyday mainichi 毎日
everything *n*. minna (all possible) 皆 nan de mo 何でも
everywhere *adv*. doko ni mo どこにも
exact *adj*. (correct) tashika na 確かな seikaku na 正確な (detailed) kuwashii 詳しい seimitsu na 精密な

examine vt. shiraberu 調べる

example n. rei 例

  for example tatoe ba たとえ
  ば

excellent adj. sugureta すぐれ
  た subarashii すばらしい

exchange vt. torikaeru 取換え
  る kōkan suru 交換する

excuse me osore irimasu 恐れ
  入ります gomen kudasai ご
  免下さい shitsurei shimasu
  失礼します

exit n. deguchi 出口

expect vt. matsu 待つ yoki suru
  予期する kitai suru 期待する

expectation n. kitai 期待 yosō
  予想

expense n. hiyō 費用

expensive adj. takai 高い

experience n. keiken 経験

explain vt. setsumei suru 説明
  する

explanation n. setsumei 説明

export n. yushutsu 輸出 vt.
  yushutsu suru 輸出する

express vt. arawasu 表す nobe-
  ru (state) 述べる n. kyūkō
  (train) 急行

extend vt. nobasu 伸ばす vi.
  nobiru 伸びる

eye n. me 目

F

face n. kao 顔

fact n. jijitsu 事実

  in fact jitsu wa 実は

factory n. kōjō 工場

fail vt. shikujiru しくじる shippai suru 失敗する

fair adj. (pretty) kirei na 綺麗
  な (clear) sunda 澄んだ

fall vi. ochiru 落ちる

false adj. uso no うその

familiar adj. shitashii 親しい
  yoku shitte iru よく知つてい
  る

family n. kazoku 家族

famous adj. yūmei na 有名な

far adj. tōi 遠い

fare n. ryōkin 料金

farmer n. hyakushō 百姓

fashion n. ryūkō 流行 hayari
  はやり

fast adj. hayai 速い

father n. chichi 父 o-tōsan
  (polite) お父さん

favor n. kōi 好意 vt. sansei
  suru 賛成する kōi o shimesu
  好意を示す

favorite n. suki na mono 好き
  なもの o-ki ni iri お気に入り
  adj. konomi no 好みの

February n. Ni-gatsu 二月

feel vt. kanjiru 感じる

feeling n. kimochi 気持

fever n. netsu 熱

few adj. sukoshi no 少しの
  adv. shōshō 少々

field n. nohara 野原

fifteen jūgo 十五

fifth day itsuka 五日

fifty go-jū 五十

film n. fuirumu フイルム

find vt. mitsukeru 見付ける

fine adj. yoi 良い ii いい rippa
  na 立派な

finger n. yubi 指

finish vi. owaru 終る vt. oeru
  終える

fire n. hi 火 kaji 火事 vi. hi ga
  tsuku 火がつく vt. hi o tsukeru 火をつける

firm n. kaisha 会社 adj. shikkari shita しっかりした

first adj. hajime no 初めの saisho no 最初の

fish *n*. sakana 魚 uo 魚

fishing tsuri 釣り

five *n*. go 五 itsutsu 五つ

flag *n*. hata 旗

flame *n*. honoo 焔 *vi*. moeru 燃える *vt*. moyasu 燃やす

flashbulb *n*. furasshu barubu フラッシュ バルブ

flavor *n*. aji 味 fūmi 風味

floor *n*. yuka 床

  first floor ikkai 一階

  second floor nikai 二階

flower *n*. hana 花

  flower arrangement ikebana 生花

following *adj*. tsugi no 次の

food *n*. tabemono 食べ物 shokumotsu 食物

fool *n*. baka 馬鹿

foot *n*. ashi 足

for *prep*. ...no tame ni ...のために

foreigner *n*. gaijin 外人

forget *vt*. wasureru 忘れる

fork *n*. fōku フォーク

forty yon-jū 四十 shi-ju 四十

forward *adv*. mae e 前へ *vt*. kaisō suru (send forward) 回送する

fountain pen *n*. mannen-hitsu 万年筆

four *n*. shi 四 yon 四 yottsu 四つ

four o'clock yoji 四時

fourteen jūshi 十四

fourth day yokka 四日

fragile *adj*. kowareyasui こわれやすい moroi もろい

frame *n*. waku 枠

France *n*. Furansu フランス

  French *adj*. Furansu no フランスの *n*. Fransujin フラン

ス人

French language Furansugo フランス語

frank *adj*. sotchoku na 卒直な

frankly *adv*. sotchoku ni 卒直に

free *adj*. jiyū na 自由な hima na (not busy) 暇な

freely *adv*. jiyū ni 自由に

frequently *adv*. shibashiba しばしば tabitabi たびたび

fresh *adj*. atarashii 新しい shinsen na 新鮮な

Friday *n*. Kin-yobi 金曜日

friend *n*. tomodachi 友達

friendly *adj*. shitashii 親しい

from *prep*. kara (*particle*) ...から

from ...to *prep*. ...kara から ...made (*particle*) ...迄

front *n*. mae 前

  in front of ...no mae ...の前

fruit *n*. kudamono 果物

full *adj*. jūbun na 充分な (detailed) kuwashii 詳しい shōsai na 詳細な

fun *n*. omoshiroi koto 面白いこと yukai na koto 愉快なこと

fund *n*. shikin 資金 shihon 資本

funny *adj*. okashii おかしい kokkei na こっけいな yukai na 愉快な omoshiroi 面白い

fur *n*. kegawa 毛皮

G

game *n*. (play) asobi 遊び (match) shiai 試合

garden *n*. niwa 庭

gasoline *n*. gasorin ガソリン

gas *n*. gasu ガス

gay *adj*. akarui 明るい yukai na 愉快な yōki na 陽気な

gentle *adj*. yasashii やさしい

gentleman *n.* shinshi 紳士

genuine *adj.* hommono no 本物の

geography *n.* chiri 地理

get *vt.* (receive) morau 貰う (have) motteiru 持っている *vi.* (become) ...ni naru になる

gift *n.* okurimono 贈り物

girl *n.* onna no ko 女の子(polite) o-jōsan お嬢さん musume 娘

give *vt.* ageru 上げる sashi-ageru (polite) 差し上げる (to me) kudasaru (polite) 下さる kureru 呉れる

glad *adj.* ureshii 嬉しい

gladly *adv.* yorokonde 喜んで

glass *n.* garasu ガラス

glasses *n.* megane 眼鏡

gloomy *adj.* yūutsu na 憂鬱な uttōshii うっとうしい

glove *n.* tebukuro 手袋

go *vi.* iku 行く yuku 行く mairu (humble) 参る

God *n.* kamisama 神様

gold *n.* kin 金

golden *adj.* kin iro no 金色の kin no 金の

gong *n.* kane 鐘

good *adj.* ii いい yoi 良い kekkō na 結構な shinsetsu na (person) 親切な

goodbye *int.* sayonara さよなら

goods *n.* shinamono 品物 shō-hin 商品

government *n.* seifu (administration) 政府 seiji 政治

gradually *adv.* dandan to だんだんと sukoshi zutsu 少しづつ shidai ni 次第に

grammar *n.* bumpō 文法

grass *n.* kusa 草

gratis *adj.* tada no 只の *adv.* tada de 只で

gray *n.* hai iro 灰色 nezumi iro ねずみ色 *adj.* hai iro no 灰色の nezumi iro no ねずみ色の

green *n.* midori 緑 ao 青 *adj.* midori no 緑の aoi 青い

greeting *n.* aisatsu 挨拶

guest *n.* kyaku 客

H

habit *n.* shūkan 習慣

hair *n.* kami 髪

haircut sampatsu 散髪

hairdresser biyōin 美容院

hair oil kami-abura 髪油

half *n.* han 半 hambun 半分

hand *n.* te 手 *vt.* (hand over) watasu 渡す

handkerchief *n.* hankachi ハンカチ

handle *n.* e 柄 *vt.* atsukau 扱う

handsome *adj.* rippa na 立派な

handy *adj.* chōhō na (convenient) 調法な benri na 便利な kiyō na (dexterous) 器用な

hang *vi.* kakatte iru 掛かっている *vt.* kakeru 掛ける tsurusu 吊す

happen *vi.* okoru 起る shōjiru 生じる

happy *adj.* ureshii 嬉しい tanoshii 楽しい

hard *adj.* (solid) katai 堅い (difficult) muzukashii むずかしい (work hard) isshōkem-mei ni 一生懸命に

harm *n.* gai 害 shōgai 傷害 *vt.* gaisuru 害する kizutsu-keru 傷つける

hat *n.* bōshi 帽子

have *vt.* aru ある motsu 持つ

hawk *n.* taka 鷹

head *n.* atama 頭 kashira (chief) 頭

health *n.* kenkō 健康

healthy *adj.* kenkō na 健康な jōbu na 丈夫な

hear *vi.* kikoeru 聞える *vt.* kiku 聞く

heart *n.* kokoro (feeling) 心 shinzō (organ) 心臓

heavy *adj.* (weight) omoi 重い (painful) tsurai 辛い (severe) hidoi ひどい

heel *n.* kakato 踵

height *n.* takasa 高さ take 丈

help *vt.* tetsudau (assist) 手伝う tasukeru (rescue) 助ける

here *adv.* koko ここ kochira こちら

high *adj.* takai 高い

history *n.* rekishi 歴史

hold *vt.* (in hand) motsu 持つ (grasp) nigiru 握る

holiday *n.* yasumi 休み

holy *adj.* shinsei na 神聖な

home *n.* taku 宅 uchi 家 katei 家庭

honest *adj.* shōjiki na 正直な

honor *n.* meiyo 名誉 kōei 光栄

hope *n.* kibō 希望 *vt.* nozomu 望む kibō suru 希望する

horrible *adj.* osoroshii 恐ろしい

hospital *n.* byōin 病院

hot *adj.* atsui 暑い

hot water (o-)yu (お)湯

hotel *n.* hoteru ホテル

hour *n.* jikan 時間

house *n.* uchi 家 ie 家

housewife *n.* shufu 主婦

how *adv.* dō どう

however *conj.* keredomo けれ ども shikashi しかし

how much *adj. adv.* ikura いくら

humid *adj.* (humidly hot) mushiatsui 蒸し暑い (damp) shimeppoi 湿っぽい

humor *n.* yūmoa ユーモア

hundred *n.* hyaku 百

hurry *vi.* isogu 急ぐ *vt.* isogaseru 急がせる *n.* ōisogi 大急ぎ

hurt *vi.* itamu 痛む *vt.* itameru 痛める

husband *n.* otto 夫 shujin 主人

husky *adj.* ganjō na 頑丈な gatchiri shita がっちりした shagareta (hoarse) しゃがれた

I

I *pron.* watakushi 私 watashi 私

my, mine watakushi no 私 の watashi no 私の

ice *n.* kōri 氷

ice cream aisu kuriimu アイスク リーム

idea *n.* kangae 考え

idiom *n.* kanyōgo 慣用語

if *conj.* moshimo もしも …naraba …ならば …nara …なら

ill *adj.* byōki no (sick) 病気の warui (evil) 悪い

illness *n.* byōki 病気

immediately *adv.* sugu ni すぐ に

immigration *n.* imin 移民

immigration office iminkyoku 移民局

import *vt.* yunyū suru 輸入する *n.* yunyū 輸入

important *adj.* jūyō na 重要な taisetsu na 大切な

impression *n.* inshō 印象

first impression daiichi inshō 第一印象

improve *vi.* yoku naru よくな

る *vt.* yoku suru よくする

in *prep.* ...ni *particle* に ...no naka ni ...の中に

include *vt.* fukumu 含む ireru 入れる

including *prep.* ...o fukumete ...を含めて

income *n.* shūnyū 収入

inconvenient *adj.* fuben na 不便な

increase *vi.* fueru 増える *vt.* fuyasu 増やす

indeed *adv.* hontō ni 本当に jitsu ni 実に naruhodo なるほど

indifferent *adj.* mukanshin na 無関心な mutonchaku na 無頓着な

industry kōgyō (manufacturing) 工業 sangyō 産業 kimben (diligence) 勤勉

inexpensive *adj.* yasui 安い

influence *n.* eikyō 影響

inform *vt.* shiraseru 知らせる

injection *n.* chūsha 注射

injury *n.* kega 怪我

inn *n.* ryokan 旅館 yadoya 宿屋

inquire *vt.* tazuneru 尋ねる toi-awasu 問い合わす

inside *prep.* ...no naka ni ...の中に

inspect *vt.* shiraberu 調べる shisatsu suru (officially) 視察する

instead *adv.* ...no kawari ni ...の代りに

insurance *n.* hoken 保険

intent *vt.* ...suru tsumori de aru ...する積りである

interesting *adj.* omoshiroi 面白い kyōmi no aru 興味のある

international *adj.* kokusai teki na 国際的な

interview *n.* menkai 面会

into *prep.* ...no naka e ...の中へ

introduction *n.* shōkai 紹介

investment *n.* shusshi 出資

invite *vt.* shōtai suru 招待する

is *vi.* desu (copula) です iru (person) いる aru (thing) ある

island *n.* shima 島

islands shimajima 島々

isn't ...dewa nai ではない ...ja nai (colloquial) ...じゃない... ja arimasen ...じゃありません

it *pron.* sore それ

J

jacket *n.* uwagi 上着

janitor *n.* kozukai 小使

January *n.* Ichi-gatsu 一月

Japan *n.* Nippon 日本

Japanese *adj.* Nippon no 日本の *n.* Nipponjin, Nihonjin 日本人

Japanese (language) Nihongo 日本語

job *n.* shigoto 仕事

joke *n.* jōdan 冗談

journey *n.* ryokō 旅行

July *n.* Shichi-gatsu 七月

June *n.* Roku-gatsu 六月

just *adj.* tadashii (right) 正しい *adv.* chōdo (exactly) ちょうど chotto (only) ちょっと

K

keep *vt.* motte iru (hold) 持っている hozon suru (preserve) 保存する azukaru (take charge of) 預かる *vi.* ...ni aru (remain) ...にある ...de iru ...でいる

key *n.* kagi 鍵

kind *adj.* (nice) shinsetsu na 親切な (variety) shurui 種類

kitchen *n.* daidokoro 台所

knee *n.* hiza 膝

knife *n.* naifu ナイフ

know *vt.* shitte iru 知つている

L

lacquer ware *n.* shikki 漆器 nuri mono 塗物

lady *n.* fujin 婦人

lake *n.* mizuumi 湖 kosui 湖水

land *n.* tochi 土地 riku (*as opp. to* sea) 陸

language *n.* kotoba 言葉 gengo 言語

lantern *n.* (paper) chōchin 提灯

lap *n.* hiza 膝

large *adj.* ōkina (big) 大きな hiroi (spacious) 広い

last *adj.* (final) saigo no 最後の (preceding) kono mae no この前の

last night yūbe 昨夜 saku ban 昨晩

late *adj.* osoi 遅い *adv.* osoku 遅く

laugh *vi.* warau 笑う

laundry *n.* sentaku 洗濯 sentakuya (shop) 洗濯屋

law *n.* hōritsu 法律

lawyer *n.* bengoshi 弁護士

learn *vt.* oboeru (commit to memory) 覚える narau (practice) 習う shiru (become aware of) 知る

leave *vt.* oite iku (depart without taking) 置いて行く oki wasureru (forget to take) 置き忘れる suteru (abandon) 捨てる deru (depart) 出る

left *n.* hidari 左

left side hidarigawa 左側

leg *n.* ashi 脚

lend *vt.* kasu 貸す

length *n.* nagasa 長さ take 丈

lens *n.* renzu レンズ

less *adj.* yori sukunai より少ない

let us ...mashō ...ましよう

letter *n.* tegami 手紙

library *n.* toshokan 図書館

life *n.* inochi 命 shōgai (the term of existence) 生がい seikatsu (way of living) 生活

light *n.* hikari 光 akari (lamp) あかり *adj.* akarui (bright) 明るい karui (not heavy) 軽い *vt.* hi o tsukeru (take fire) 火をつける terasu (illuminate) 照らす

like *vt.* suku 好く *adj.* (similar to) ...niteiru ...に似ている

line *n.* sen 線

liquor *n.* sake 酒

list *n.* hyō 表 (make a list) hyō ni suru 表にする

listen *vi.* kiku 聞く

literature *n.* bungaku 文学

little *adj.* chiisai 小さい (quantity) sukoshi 少し

live *vi.* sunde iru 住んでいる

long *adj.* nagai 長い

look *vt.* miru 見る

lose *vt.* nakusu 無くす ushinau 失う

get lost michi ni mayou 道に迷う

lotus *n.* hasu 蓮

loud *adj.* ōgoe no (voice) 大声の yakamashii (noisy) やかましい hade na (showy) 派手な *adv.* ōgoe de (voice) 大声で

love *n.* ai (affection) 愛 koi (sexual affection) 恋 *vt.* ai suru 愛する ai shimasu

(polite) 愛します
love letter koibumi 恋文
low *adj.* hikui 低い
lucky *adj.* un ga ii 運がいい
lunch *n.* hirugohan 昼御飯
luxurious *adj.* zeitaku na 贅沢
な

M

machine *n.* kikai 機械
magazine *n.* zasshi 雑誌
maid *n.* jochu 女中
mail *n.* yūbin 郵便
  air mail kōkū yūbin 航空郵便
  sea (**surface**) **mail** funa bin
船便
mailbox posuto ポスト
mailman yūbin haitatsunin
郵便配達人 yūbin-ya 郵便屋
main *adj.* omo na 主な
make *vt.* tsukuru 作る koshi-
raeru こしらえる naru (deve-
lop into) なる
man *n.* otoko (male) 男 hito
(human) 人
manicure *n.* manikyua マニキ
ュア
manner *n.* (method) hōhō 方法
yarikata やり方 (attitude) 態
度
manners gyōgi 行儀 okonai 行
い
many *adj.* takusan no 沢山の
ōku no 多くの
map *n.* chizu 地図
March *n.* San-gatsu 三月
market *n.* ichiba 市場 shijo 市場
marriage *n.* kekkon 結婚
marry *vt.* kekkon suru 結婚す
る
match *n.* (game) shiai 試合
(for fire) matchi マッチ
materials *n.* zairyō 材料 shiryō

資料
(for clothes) kiji 布地
May *n.* Go-gatsu 五月
may *aux. v.* ...ka mo shirenai
...かも知れない (permission)
...te mo ii ...てもいい
maybe *adv.* tabun 多分 osoraku 恐らく
meal *n.* shokuji 食事
meaning *n.* imi 意味
meat *n.* niku 肉
medicine *n.* kusuri 薬
meet *vt.* au 会う
mend *vt.* naosu 直す tsukurou
つくろう
menu *n.* kondate 献立 menyū
メニュー
merchandise *n.* shōshin 商品
merchant *n.* shōnin 商人
merry *adj.* yōki na 陽気な
message *n.* kotozuke 言づけ dengon 伝言
meter *n.* mētoru メートル mētā
(for taxi) メーター
method *n.* hōhō 方法
middle *n.* chūō 中央 mannaka
真中 *adj.* chūō no 中央の
mannaka no 真中の
middle age *n.* chūnen 中年
middle-aged *adj.* chūnen no 中
年の
mine *pron.* watakushi no mono
私のもの
ministry *n.* shō 省
Ministry of Education
mombushō 文部省
Ministry of Finance
ōkurashō 大蔵省
Ministry of Foreign Affairs
gaimushō 外務省
Ministry of Postal Services
yūseishō 郵政省 etc.
minute *n.* fun 分
  one minute ip-pun 一分

two minutes nifun 二分
mirror n. kagami 鏡
Miss, Mrs., Mr. n. san さん
missile n. misairu ミサイル
mistake n. machigai 間違い vt. machigaeru 間違える
misunderstand vt. gokai suru 誤解する
mix vi. mazaru 混ざる vt. mazeru 混ぜる
mold n. kabi かび
moment n. shunkan (instant) 瞬間 toki (time) 時 baai (occasion) 場合
   at any moment itsu demo 何時でも
   at this moment ima 今
   for a moment chotto no aida ちょっとの 間
   for the moment sashiatari さし当り
   in a moment sugu ni すぐに
   just a moment chotto matte kudasai　ちょつと待つて下さい
Monday n. Getsu-yōbi 月曜日
money n. (o-) kane （お）金
   money order kawase 為替
month n. tsuki 月 …kagetsu …カ月
   every month tsukizuki 月々
more adj. motto もつと
morning n. asa 朝
   good morning ohayō gozaimasu お早ようございます
most adj. mottomo 最も ……na ichiban ……na 一番……な taitei no (nearly all) たいていの adv. mottomo 最も ichiban 一番
mother n. haha 母 okāsan お母さん okāsama (polite) お母様

motorcycle n. ōtobai オートバイ
mountain n. yama 山
mouth n. kuchi 口
mushroom n. kinoko きのこ
move vi. ugoku 動く vt. ugokasu 動かす (change one's residence) hikkosu 引越す
movies n. eiga 映画
movie theater eiga-kan 映画館
Mrs., Mr. n. san さん
much adv. takusan 沢山 adj. takusan no 沢山の
museum n. hakubutsukan 博物館 bijutsukan (art) 美術館
music n. ongaku 音楽
my pron. watakushi no 私の

N

nail n. tsume 爪
name n. namae 名前
name plate : hyōsatsu 標札
nap n. hirune 昼寝
narrow adj. semai 狭い
nasty adj. iyana いやな
nature n. shizen 自然 seishitsu (character) 性質
near adj. chikai 近い
nearest moyori no 最寄の
nearly adv. hotondo 殆んど oyoso およそ
neat adj. sappari shita さっぱりした kichin to shita きちんとした
necessary adj. hitsuyō na 必要な
neck n. kubi 首
necklace kubikazari 頸飾り
necktie n. nekutai ネクタイ
need vt. iru 要る
needle n. hari 針
neglect vi. mushi suru 無視する
neither …nor… conj. …de mo nakereba …de mo nai …でもなければ …でもない
nephew n. oi 甥

never *adv*. kesshite ...nai 決して...ない

new *adj*. atarashii 新しい

newspaper *n*. shimbun 新聞

next *adj*. tsugi no 次の
next week raishū 来週
next year rainen 来年

nice *adj*. ii いい yoi 良い kekkō na 結構な

niece *n*. mei 姪

night *n*. yoru 夜

nine *n*. ku 九 kokonotsu 九つ

nineteen jūkyū 十九 jūku 十九

ninety kyū-jū 九十 ku-jū 九十

ninth day kokonoka 九日

no *int*. iie いいえ

noisy *adj*. yakamashii やかましい sōzōshii 騒々しい

noodles *n*. soba そば udon うどん

noodle shop soba-ya そばや udon-ya うどんや

noon *n*. hiru 昼

north *n*. kita 北

nose *n*. hana 鼻

note *n*. shirushi (mark) しるし oboegaki (memorandum) 覚書 chū (explanatory comment) 注 tegami (letter) 手紙 oto (tone) 音

novel *n*. shōsetsu 小説

November *n*. Jūichi-gatsu 十一月

now *adv*. ima 今 tadaima 只今

O

object *n*. (thing) mono 物 (goal) mokuteki 目的 *vt*. hantai suru 反対する

observation *n*. kansatsu 観察 shisatsu 視察

occasionally *adv*. tokidoki 時々 oriori 折々

Occident *n*. Seiyō 西洋

occupation (job) shokugyō 職業

ocean *n*. umi 海

October *n*. Jū-gatsu 十月

odd (queer) hen na 変な (left-over) nokori no 残りの amatta 余つた

odor *n*. nioi におい kaori 香り

of *prep*. ...no ...の

office *n*. jimusho 事務所
office worker jimuin 事務員

official *n*. yakunin (government) 役人

often *adv*. yoku よく tabitabi 度々 shibashiba しばしば

old *adj*. (not new) furui 古い (not young) toshi yori no 年寄りの

older toshiue no 年上の

omelet *n*. omuretsu オムレツ

omit *vt*. habuku 省く nukasu ぬかす

on *prep*. ...ni (*particle*) ...に...no ue ni ...の上に

once *adv*. ichi-do 一度 ikkai 一回

one *n*. ichi 一 hitotsu 一つ
eleven jūichi 十一
one person hitori 一人
first day tsuitachi 一日

onion *n*. tamanegi たまねぎ

only *adv*. ...dake だけ ...tada ...只

open *vi*. aku 開く *vt*. akeru 開ける

operation *n*. (action) hataraki 働き sagyō 作業 (medical) shujutsu 手術

operator (telephone) *n*. kōkan-shu 交換手 denwa kōkan-shu 電話交換手

opinion *n*. kangae 考え iken 意見

opportunity n. kikai 機会

opposite adj. mukaigawa no (front) 向い側の hantai no (contrary) 反対の

or conj. mata wa 又は soretomo それとも arui wa 或は

order n. meirei (command) 命令 chūmon (for purchase) 注文 junjo (sequence) 順序 vt. meirei suru 命令する chūmon suru 注文する

in order to ...suru tame ni するために

ordinary adj. futsū no 普通の

organization n. (set up) soshiki 組織 (group) dantai 団体

other adj. hokano ほかの betsu no 別の

out adv. soto e 外え soto ni 外に

out of house rusu desu 留守です

over prep. (above) ...no ue ni ...の上に (beyond) ...o koete ...を越えて ...no mukō ni ...の向うに (too far) ...sugiru ...過ぎる

P

package n. kozutsumi 小包

pain n. itami 痛み vi. itamu 痛む

paper n. kami 紙

papers shorui 書類

parcel n. kozutsumi 小包

pardon me osore irimasu 恐れ入ります gomen kudasai ご免下さい shitsurei shimasu 失礼します

parent n. oya 親

parents ryōshin 両親

park n. kōen 公園

part n. bubun 部分

particular adj. tokubetsu no 特別の

pass vt. (go past) tōru 通る (hand over) watasu 渡す vi. (time passes) tatsu 経つ

past adj. kako no 過去の n. kako 過去 mukashi 昔 prep. ...sugi (after) 過ぎ

paste n. nori 糊

patent n. tokkyoken 特許権

path n. kōji 小路

patient adj. shimbōzuyoi 辛抱強い konki no yoi 根気のよい

pay vt. harau 払う shiharau 支払う

peace n. heiwa 平和

pear n. nashi 梨

pearl n. shinju 真珠

pedal n. pedaru ペダル

peel vt. muku むく

pencil n. empitsu 鉛筆

people n. hitobito 人々 kokumin (nation) 国民

pepper n. koshō 胡椒

per prep. ...ni tsuki ...に付 ...goto ni ...ごとに ...tai ...対

percent n. pāssento パーセント

perfect adj. kanzen na 完全な

performance n. ensō (music) 演奏 engi (action) 演技 kōgyō (show) 興業

perfume n. kōsui 香水

perhaps adv. tabun 多分 osoraku 恐らく

period n. kikan 期間

periodic adj. teiki no 定期の

permission n. kyoka 許可

person n. hito 人

one person hitori 一人

three persons san-nin 三人

perspiration n. ase 汗

perspire vi. ase o kaku 汗をかく

pickpocket *n.* suri すり

picture *n.* e 絵 (photograph) shashin 写真

pill *n.* ganyaku 丸薬

pillow *n.* makura 枕

pity *n.* awaremi 憐み *vt.* kawaisō ni omou 可哀そうに思う awaremu 憐む

place *n.* tokoro 所 basho 場所

plan *n.* keikaku 計画 *vt.* (intend to) ...tsumori desu ...つもりです

plate *n.* sara 皿

play *vi.* asobu 遊ぶ *vt.* suru する tanoshimu (game) たのしむ enzuru (drama) 演ずる ensō suru (music) 演奏する *n.* asobi (game) 遊び shibai (drama) 芝居

plaza *n.* hiroba 広場

pleasant *adj.* tanoshii 楽しい yukai na 愉快な omoshiroi 面白い

please *vt.* yorokobasu 喜ばす dōzo (may it please you)どうぞ kudasai 下さい

p. m. gogo 午後

poem *n.* shi 詩

poet *n.* shijin 詩人

point *n.* ten (dot, spot) 点 saki (tip) 先 *vt.* togarasu (sharpen) とがらす *vi.* yubi sasu 指さす

police *n.* keisatsu 警察

policeman junsa 巡査

polite *adj.* teinei na 丁寧な

politics *n.* seiji 政治

pond *n.* ike 池

poor *adj.* mazushii (needy) 貧しい heta na (unskillful) 下手な warui (bad) 悪い

popular *adj.* ninki ga aru (regarded with favor) 人気がある hayaru (prevailing) はやる

population *n.* jinkō 人口

porch *n.* genkan 玄関

port *n.* minato 港

porter *n.* (at stations) akabō 赤帽

pose *n.* shisei 姿勢

possible *adj.* dekiru (feasible) 出来る ari sō na (thinkable) ありそうな

　if possible dekiru koto nara 出来る事なら

post card *n.* hagaki 葉書

　picture post card e-hagaki 絵葉書

post office *n.* yūbinkyoku 郵便局

postpone *vt.* enki suru 延期する

postponement *n.* enki 延期

pound *n.* pondo ポンド

powder *n.* kona 粉 o-shiroi (cosmetic powder) お白粉

practice *n.* renshū 練習 *vt.* renshū suru 練習する

praise *vt.* homeru 褒める

preceding *adj.* mae no 前の

precious *adj.* kichō na 貴重な daiji na 大事な

prefer *vt.* ...no hō o konomu ...の方を好む

preparation *n.* jumbi 準備

press *vt.* osu 押す *vi.* airon o kakeru (iron) アイロンをかける

pretty *adj.* kirei na 綺麗な

price *n.* nedan 値段

pride *n.* hokori 誇り

private *adj.* watakushi no 私の kojin no 個人の shiritsu no (*opp. to* public) 私立の

probably *adv.* tabun 多分 osoraku 恐らく

problem *n.* mondai 問題

produce *vt.* (industry) seisan suru 生産する (play, etc.) jōen susu 上演する

product *n.* sambutsu 産物

promise *n.* yakusoku 約束 *vt.* yakusoku suru 約束する

promising *adj.* yūbō no 有望な

prompt *adj.* hayai 早い

propaganda *n.* senden 宣伝

proper *adj.* tekitō na 適当な

prose *n.* sambun 散文

prospect *n.* (of scenery) mihara-shi 見晴し (of future) mitō-shi 見通し

prove *vt.* shōmei suru 証明する *vi.* de aru koto ga wakaru であることがわかる

proverb *n.* kotowaza 諺

public *adj.* kōshū no 公衆の ōyake no (*opp. to* private) 公の *n.* kokumin (people) 国民

pull *vt.* hiku 引く

purchase *vt.* kau 買う

pure *adj.* junsui na 純粋な

purple *adj.* murasaki iro no 紫色の *n.* murasaki iro 紫色

purpose *n.* (goal) mokuteki 目的 (intension) tsumori つもり
  for the purpose of ...no tame ni ...のために
  on purpose waza to わざと

purse *n.* saifu 財布

push *vt.* osu 押す

put *vt.* oku 置く

Q

qualification *n.* (stipulation) jō-ken 条件 (competency) shi-kaku 資格

quality *n.* shitsu 質 hinshitsu 品質

quantity *n.* ryō 量 bunryō 分量

quarrel *n.* kenka 喧嘩 *vi.* ken-ka suru 喧嘩する

question *n.* shitsumon (interro-gation) 質問 gimon (inquiry) 疑問 *vt.* shitsumon suru 質問する gimon o okosu 疑問を起す

quick *adj.* hayai 早い

quiet *adj.* shizuka na 静かな

quilt *n.* futon ふとん

quite *adv.* sōtō (considerably) 相当 daibu 大分 sukkari (en-tirely) すっかり

quote *vt.* in-yō suru 引用する

R

racket *n.* raketto ラケット

radio *n.* rajio ラヂオ

railway *n.* tetsudō 鉄道

rain *n.* ame 雨 *vi.* ame ga furu 雨が降る

raincoat rein-kōto レインコート

rapid *adj.* hayai 早い subayai すばやい

rare *adj.* (unusual) mezurashii 珍しい (food) namayake no 生焼けの namanie no 生煮えの

rate *n.* wariai (ratio) 割合 sōba 相場 nedan (price) 値段 ryō-kin (fare) 料金

razor *n.* kamisori かみそり
  razor blade kamisori no ha かみそりの刃

reach *vt.* tsuku 着く todoku 届く

read *vt.* yomu 読む

ready *adj.* jumbi no dekita 準備の出来た

realize *vt.* wakaru 分る (materi-alize) jitsugen suru 実現する

really *adv.* hontō ni 本当に

reason *n.* riyū 理由 wake わけ

receipt *n.* uketori 受取

receive vt. uketoru 受取る itadaku (humble) 頂く chōdaisuru (humble) 頂戴する

recently adv. saikin 最近 chika goro 近頃 kono goro この頃

recognize vt. mitomeru 認める shōnin suru (acknowledge) 承認する

recommend vt. susumeru 勧める suisen suru 推薦する

recover vi. (from illness) naoru 治る kaifuku suru 回復する

recreation n. goraku 娯楽

red adj. akai 赤い n. aka 赤

refer vi. toiawasu (go for information) 問合わす shōkai suru 照会する

reference n. toiawasu 問合せ shōkai 照会 shōmeisho (testimonial) 証明書

refined adj. (decent) jōhin na 上品な

refuse vt. kotowaru 断る

regard n. kanshin 関心 kankei 関係
　give my regards to... ...ni yoroshiku ...によろしく
　in regard to ...ni tsuite ...について
　with regard to ...ni kanshite ...に関して

registration n. tōroku 登録

regular adj. teiki no (periodic) 定期の futsū no (usual) 普通の

relax vt. yurumeru (loosen) ゆるめる kutsurogu (put oneself at ease) 寛ぐ vi. yawaragu (become less severe) 和ぐ

religion n. shūkyō 宗教

remain vi. nokoru 残る n. nokori 残り

remember vt. omoidasu (recollect) 思い出す oboeteiru (bear in mind) 覚えている

remind vt. omowaseru 思わせる omoidasaseru 思い出させる

rent vt. kariru (from) 借りる vi. kasu (to) 貸す

repair vt. naosu 直す shūzen suru 修繕する

report vt. shiraseru 知らせる hōkoku suru 報告する

reporter kisha 記者

request vi. tanomu 頼む negau 願う n. yōkyū 要求 tanomi 頼み negai 願い

require vt. hitsuyō to suru 必要とする iru 要る

resemble vt. nite iru 似ている

reservation n. (rooms, seats, etc.) yoyaku 予約

resin n. yani やに

responsibility n. sekinin 責任 tsutome 務め

rest vi. yasumu 休む n. nokori (remainder) 残り

result n. kekka 結果

return vi. kaeru 帰る modoru 戻る vt. modosu (put back) 戻す

reverse vt. hantai ni suru 反対にする uragaesu (turn inside out) 裏返す vi. hantai ni naru 反対になる n. hantai 反対 gyaku 逆 adj. hantai no 反対の gyaku no 逆の

rice n. kome 米 gohan (cooked) 御飯

rich adj. kanemochi no 金持の yutaka na (abundant) 豊かな

ride vi. noru 乗る

right n. migi 右

right side migigawa 右側 adj. tadashii (correct) 正しい migi no 右の

ring *n.* (on finger) yubiwa 指輪

rise *vi.* (get up) okiru 起きる (go up) agaru 上がる (climb) noboru 昇る (sun, moon, etc.) deru 出る

river *n.* kawa 川, 河

road *n.* michi 道 dōro 道路

robber *n.* dorobō 泥棒

rock *n.* iwa 岩

roll *vi.* korogaru ころがる *vt.* korogasu ころがす

Romanization *n.* Rōmaji ローマ字

roof *n.* yane 屋根

room *n.* heya 部屋

root *n.* (of grasses, trees) ne 根 (of hair, teeth, nails, fingers) nemoto 根元 (foundation) kiso 基礎 (basic element) honshitsu 本質

rope *n.* tsuna 綱 nawa 縄

rose *n.* bara ばら

rough *adj.* arai 粗い rambō na (violent) 乱暴な

round *adj.* marui 円い

rude *adj.* shitsurei na 失礼な

ruin *vt.* dame ni suru 駄目にする dainashi ni suru 台なしにする

rumor *n.* uwasa うわさ

run *vi.* hashiru 走る kakeru 駆ける

rush *vi.* isogu 急ぐ

Russia *n.* Roshiya ロシヤ

Russian *adj.* Roshiya no ロシヤの Roshiyajin (people) ロシヤ人 Roshiyago (language) ロシヤ語

S

sack *n.* fukuro 袋

sacred *adj.* shinsei na 神聖な

sacrifice *n.* gisei 犠牲

sad *adj.* kanashii 悲しい

safe buji na 無事な anzen na 安全な

sake *n.* tame (consideration) ため

for the sake of ...no tame ni のために

salary *n.* (usually monthly) gekkyū 月給 kyūryō 給料

salt *n.* shio 塩

same *adj.* onaji 同じ

sample *n.* mihon 見本

sand *n.* suna 砂

sandwich *n.* sandoitchi サンドイッチ

sash *n.* obi 帯

satire *n.* fūshi 諷刺 hiniku 皮肉

satisfy *vt.* manzoku saseru 満足させる

be satisfied manzoku suru 満足する

Saturday *n.* Do-yōbi 土曜日

saucer *n.* ukezara 受皿

save *vt.* sukuu (rescue) 救う setsuyaku suru (economize) 節約する takuwaeru (lay by) 貯える

say *vt.* iu 言う

scale *n.* uroko (of fish) うろこ hakari (weighing machine) はかり monosashi (measure) 物さし kibo (of business, etc.) 規模

scarce *adj.* sukunai 少い mare na 稀な

scare *vi.* odoroku 驚く *vt.* odorokasu 驚かす odosu おどす

scenery *n.* keshiki 景色

scent *n.* kaori かおり nioi におい

schedule *n.* mokuroku (catalogue) 目録 meisaisho (of bill) 明細書 (timetable) jikanhyō

時間表

scheme *n.* (plan) keikaku 計画 (system) soshiki 組織

scholar *n.* gakusha 学者

school *n.* gakkō 学校
  schoolteacher sensei 先生 kyōshi 教師

science *n.* kagaku 科学

scissors *n.* hasami はさみ

scope *n.* yochi 余地 (room) han-i (range) 範囲

score *n.* sukoa スコア

screen *n.* byōbu びょうぶ tsuitate ついたて sukurin (movie) スクリン

scroll *n.* makimono 巻物

sculpture *n.* chōkoku 彫刻

sea *n.* umi 海
  sea mail funa bin 船便
  seasickness funayoi 船酔い
  seashore kaigan 海岸

seal *n.* (for stamping one's name) han 判

search *vt.* sagasu 探す

season *n.* kisetsu 季節
  four seasons shiki 四季

seasoning *n.* (of food) chōmiryō 調味料

seat *n.* seki 席

second day futsuka 二日

secret *adj.* himitsu no 秘密の naisho no 内証の

see *vt.* miru (meet) 見る au 会う

seek *vt.* sagasu 探す

seem *vi.* ...rashii ...らしい

seldom *adv.* metta ni めったに

select *vt.* erabu 選ぶ

self *n.* jishin 自身

sell *vt.* uru 売る

send *vt.* okuru 送る (telegram) utsu 打つ (person) ikaseru 行かせる

separate *adj.* (different) betsu no 別の *vi.* wakareru 分れる *vt.* wakeru 分ける

September *n.* Ku-gatsu 九月

serene *adj.* (sky, etc.) sumiwatatta 澄み渡った (sea, etc.) no doka na のどかな odayaka na 穏やかな (life, etc.) heiwa na 平和な (face, nature of a man) ochitsuita 落着いた

serious *adj.* majime na まじめな

serve *vi.* tsukaeru (act as a servant) 仕える (o-)kyūji suru (wait at table) (お)給仕する yaku ni tatsu (be of use) 役に立つ

set *vt.* oku (place) 置く *vi.* shizumu (sink...sun) 沈む *n.* kumi (collection) 組 setto (hairdressing) セット

settle *vi.* (down) ochitsuku 落着く (into shape) mehana ga tsuku 目鼻がつく

seven *n.* shichi 七 nanatsu 七つ

seventeen jū-shichi 十七

seventh day nanoka 七日

seventy shichi-jū 七十 nana-jū 七十

several *adj.* jakkan 若干 ikutsuka いくつか

sew *vt.* nuu 縫う

shade *n.* kage 蔭, 陰

shake *vi.* yureru 揺れる *vt.* yusuburu ゆすぶる furu 振る
  shake hands akushu suru 握手する

shallow *adj.* asai 浅い

shame *n.* haji 恥
  That's a shame sore wa ikemasen ne. それはいけませんね

shape *n.* katachi 形

sharp *adj.* surudoi 鋭い (clever) rikō na 利口な (clear) hakki-ri shita はっきりした

shave *vi.* hige o soru ひげをそる

sheet *n.* shikifu 敷布 ichimai (paper) 一枚

shelf *n.* tana 棚

shift *vt.* kaeru 変える henkō suru 変更する *vi.* kawaru 変る *n.* iten (transfer) 移転 kō-tai (working schedule) 交代

shine *vi.* kagayaku 輝く teru (sun) 照る *vt.* migaku (polish) 磨く

ship *n.* fune 船

shirt *n.* waishatsu ワイシャツ

shiver *vi.* furueru 震える

shoehorn kutsubera 靴べら

shoelaces kutsuhimo 靴ひも

shoemaker kutsuya 靴屋

shoes *n.* kutsu 靴

shoeshine kutsumigaki 靴磨き

shop mise 店

shopping *n.* kaimono 買物

short *adj.* (not long) mijikai 短い (not tall) hikui 低い

shortcut *n.* chikamichi 近道

shoulder *n.* kata 肩

show *vi.* mieru 見える *vt.* mi-seru 見せる *n.* shibai (play) 芝居

shower *n.* (of bath) shawā シャワー (rainfall) yūdachi 夕立

shrewd *adj.* chakkari shita ちゃっかりした

shrine *n.* jinja 神社 jingū 神宮

shrink *vi.* chijimu 縮む

shut *vi.* shimaru 締まる *vt.* shimeru 締める

sickness *n.* byōki 病気

sick person byōnin 病人

side *n.* yoko 横 (of body) waki わき

that side achira gawa あちら側

this side kochira gawa こちら側

which side dochira gawa どちら側

both sides ryōgawa 両側

sidewalk *n.* hodō 歩道 jindō 人道

sightseeing *n.* kembutsu 見物 kankō 観光

sign *n.* shirushi (indication, mark) しるし aizu (signal) 合図 kamban (signboard) 看板 *vt.* shomei suru 署名する

signal *n.* shingō 信号

silent *adj.* shizuka na 静かな shin to shita しんとした

silk *n.* kinu 絹

silver *n.* gin 銀 *adj.* gin no 銀の gin iro no (color) 銀色の

similar *adj.* dōyō no 同様の …niteiru 似ている

simple *adj.* kantan na 簡単な tanjun na 単純な

since *conj.* …kara …から …node …ので *prep.* …irai …以来

sincere *adj.* seijitsu na 誠実な

sing *vt.* utau 歌う

single *adj.* (for one person) hitori no 一人の (unmarried) dokushin 独身 (room) koshitsu 個室

sister *n.* shimai, kyōdai (same characters) 姉妹

elder sister ane 姉 onē san (polite) お姉さん

younger sister imōto 妹

sit *vi.* suwaru 坐る

six *n.* roku 六 muttsu 六つ

sixteen jū-roku 十六
sixth day muika 六日
sixty roku-jū 六十
size *n.* ōkisa 大きさ
skating *n.* skēto スケート
skin *n.* (of living creatures) hifu 皮膚 (of others) kawa 皮
skirt *n.* sukāto スカート
sky *n.* sora 空
sleep *vi.* nemuru 眠る neru 寝る
sleepy *adj.* nemui 眠い
sleeve *n.* sode 袖
slice *n.* hitokire 一切れ
slight *adj.* sukoshi no 少しの wazuka na わずかな
slow *adj.* osoi 遅い yukkuri ゆっくり
small *adj.* chiisai 小さい chiisana 小さな (short) hikui 低い
smile *vi.* hohoemu ほほえむ nikoniko suru にこにこする *n.* hohoemi ほほえみ
smoke *n.* kemuri 煙 *vi.* (cigarette) tabako o suu タバコを吸う
　no smoking kin-en 禁煙
snack *n.* oyatsu おやつ
sneeze *n.* kushami くしゃみ *vi.* kushami o suru くしゃみをする
snore *n.* ibiki いびき *vi.* ibiki o kaku いびきをかく
snow yuki 雪 *vi.* yuki ga furu 雪が降る
so *adv.* sō そう
　Is that so? Sō desu ka? そうですか
soap *n.* sekken 石鹸
socialism *n.* shakaishugi 社会主義
society *n.* shakai 社会 (associa-

tions) kyōkai 協会
socks *n.* kutsushita 靴下
soft *adj.* yawarakai 柔らかい
solid *adj.* (hard) katai 固い (strong) jōbu na 丈夫な gatchiri shita がっちりした
some *adj.* (a little) sukoshi 少し shōshō 少々 ikuraka いくらか (particular) aru ある
somebody *pron.* dareka 誰か
something *pron.* nanika 何か
sometime *adv.* itsuka いつか
sometimes *adv.* tokidoki 時々
somewhere *adv.* dokoka 何処か
son *n.* musuko 息子
song *n.* uta 歌
soon *adv.* sugu すぐ mamonaku 間もなく
sorry *adj.* zannen desu 残念です o ki no doku desu お気の毒です
　I am sorry dōmo sumimasen どうもすみません dōmo shitsurei shimashita どうも失礼しました
sort *n.* shurui 種類
soup *n.* sūpu スープ
south *n.* minami 南
speak *vi.* hanasu 話す mōsu 申す
special *adj.* tokubetsu no 特別の
spell *vt.* (words) ji o tsuzuru 字を綴る
spend *vt.* (money) tsukau 使う (time) sugosu 過す
spirit *n.* seishin 精神 kokoro 心
spit *vi.* tsuba o haku つばを吐く
splendid *adj.* rippa na 立派な
split *vi.* wareru 割れる *vt.* waru 割る
spoil *vi.* waruku naru 悪くなる *vt.* waruku suru 悪くする

spoon *n.* spūn スプーン

sports *n.* spōtsu スポーツ

spot *n.* ten 点

spread *vi.* hirogaru 広がる nobiru 伸びる *vt.* hirogeru 広げる nobasu 伸ばす

spring *n.* (season) haru 春
　hot spring onsen 温泉

square *n.* shikaku 四角 *adj.* shikaku no 四角の

stage *n.* butai (of a theater) 舞台 dankai (period of development) 段階 *vt.* jōen suru (put on the stage) 上演する

stairs *n.* kaidan 階段

stamp *n.* kitte 切手

stand *vi.* tatsu 立つ

standard *n.* hyōjun (criterion) 標準 *adj.* hyōjun no 標準の

star *n.* hoshi 星

starch *n.* dempun 澱粉 nori (used to stiffen linen, etc.) 糊

start *vt.* (work) hajimeru 始める *vi.* (train) shuppatsu suru 出発する

stateroom *n.* senshitsu 船室

station *n.* eki 駅

stationery *n.* binsen 便箋

stay *vi.* taizai suru 滞在する tomaru 泊まる oru 居る

steadily *adv.* chaku chaku to 着々と

steak *n.* sutēki ステーキ

step *n.* ayumi 歩み hitoashi (distance) ひと足 ashioto (footstep) 足音 kaidan (stairs) 階段 *vi.* aruku 歩く

stew *n.* shichū シチュー

still *adv.* (as yet) mada まだ nao なお

stocking *n.* sutokkingu ストッキング

stone *n.* ishi 石

stop *vi.* tomaru 止まる yamu 止む *vt.* tomeru 止める yameru 止める

store *n.* mise 店 toraiki トライキ

storm *n.* arashi 嵐

story *n.* hanashi 話

straight *adj.* massugu na 真直ぐな *adv.* massugu ni 真直ぐに

strange *adj.* hen na 変な

street *n.* michi 道 tōri 通り

strength *n.* chikara 力 tsuyosa 強さ

stretch *vi.* nobiru 伸びる *vt.* nobasu 伸ばす

strict *adj.* genkaku na 厳格な

strike *n.* (walkout) sutoraiki スト

string *n.* himo 紐

strong *adj.* tsuyoi 強い

stubborn *adj.* ganko na 頑固な

student *n.* gakusei 学生

study *vt.* benkyō suru 勉強する kenkyū suru 研究する *n.* benkyō 勉強 kenkyū 研究 shosai (room) 書斎

suburb *n.* kōgai 郊外

subway *n.* chikatetsu 地下鉄

success *n.* seikō 成功

such *adj.* sonna そんな sonoyō na そのような

suddenly *adv.* totsuzen 突然

sugar *n.* satō 砂糖

suggest *vt.* teian suru 提案する

suit *n.* (man's clothes) sebiro 背広 (woman's clothes) sūtsu スーツ
　suitcase sūtsu kēsu スーツケース

suitable *adj.* fusawashii ふさわしい niau 似合う

summer *n.* natsu 夏

sun *n.* hi 陽 taiyō 太陽

Sunday *n.* Nichi-yōbi 日曜日

superstition *n.* meishin 迷信

supper *n.* yū han 夕飯 yū shoku 夕食

support *vt.* (approve) sanseisuru 賛成する shiji suru 支持する yashinau (maintain) 養う

sure *adj.* tashika na 確かな

surprise *vt.* bikkuri saseru びっくりさせる

    be surprised odoroku 驚く

sweet *adj.* (taste) amai 甘い (lovely) kawaii 可愛い、(kind) shinsetsu na 親切な

swim oyogu 泳ぐ

swimming suiei 水泳

sympathize *vi.* dōjō suru 同情する

system *n.* (setup) soshiki 組織 (institution) seido 制度

T

table *n.* tēburu テーブル

tail *n.* o 尾 shippo しっぽ

tailor *n.* yōfukuya 洋服屋

take *vt.* toru 取る motte iku (carry) 持って行く noru (car, bus, etc.) 乗る

talk *vi.* hanasu 話す

tall *adj.* takai 高い

tangerine *n.* mikan 蜜柑

tariff *n.* kanzei 関税

task *n.* shigoto 仕事

    home task shukudai 宿題

taste *n.* aji 味 fūmi 風味 *vt.* ajiwau 味う

tax *n.* zeikin 税金

taxi *n.* takushii タクシー

tea *n.* cha 茶 o-cha (polite) お茶

    tea ceremony, tea cult cha-no-yu 茶の湯

teach *vt.* oshieru 教える

team *n.* chiimu チーム

tear *n.* hokorobi 綻び sakeme

裂け目 *vi.* sakeru 裂ける *vt.* saku 裂く

telegram *n.* dempō 電報

telephone *n.* denwa 電話

    telephone operator denwa kōkanshu 電話交換手

telescope *n.* bōenkyō 望遠鏡

television *n.* terebi テレビ

tell *vt.* iu 言う hanasu 話す mōsu 申す

temple *n.* (o-)tera (お)寺

ten *n.* jū 十 tō 十

tenth day tōka 十日

terminal *n.* shūten 終点

tennis court *n.* tenisu kōto テニスコート

terrible *adj.* hidoi (tremendous) ひどい、osoroshii (fearful) 恐ろしい

than *conj.* ...yori ...より

thank *vt.* kansha suru 感謝する o-rei o iu お礼を云う

    Thank you arigatō gozaimasu 有難うございます

that *adj.* sono その (over there) ano あの

    that one sore それ (over there) are あれ *pron.* sore それ

theater *n.* (building) gekijo 劇場 (play) shibai 芝居

then *adv.* (after that) sore kara それから (in that case) sore dewa それでは

there *adv.* soko そこ (over there) asoko あそこ asuko あすこ

    there is ...ga aru ...がある

therefore *adv.* dakara だから

thick *adj.* atsui 厚い、(round) futoi 太い

thief *n.* dorobō 泥棒

thin *adj.* usui 薄い hosoi (round) 細い

thing *n.* mono 物 (fact) koto 事

think *vt. vi.* omou 思う kan-

gaeru 考える
third day mikka 三日
thirteen jūsan 十三
thirty sanjū 三十
this *adj.* kono この
   this one kore これ *pron.* kore これ
thorough *adj.* jūbun na 十分な kanzen na 完全な
though *conj.* de mo でも *adv.* yahari やはり
thought *n.* kangae 考え
thousand *n.* sen 千
thread *n.* ito 糸
three *n.* san 三 mittsu 三つ
throat *n.* nodo 喉
through *prep.* (putting)...o tōshite ...を通して (coming) ...o tōtte ...を通って (seeing) ...no aida kara ...の間から (by means of) ...o tsukatte ...を使って
throw *vt.* nageru 投げる
Thursday *n.* Moku-yōbi 木曜日
ticket *n.* kippu 切符
tie *vt.* musubu 結ぶ yuwaeru ゆわえる *n.* nekutai (necktie) ネクタイ
tight *adj.* (narrow) kitsui きつい (firm) katai 堅い (rigid) kyūkutsu na 窮屈な
time *n.* toki 時 (hour) jikan 時間 (leisure) hima 暇
tip *n.* chippu チップ
tired of akiru 飽きる
tired with tsukareru 疲れる
to *prep.* ...ni ...に ...e ...へ
today *n.* kyō 今日
together *adv.* issho ni 一緒に
toilet *n.* benjo 便所 (polite) gofujō ご不浄 otearai お手洗い

toilet paper chirigami 塵紙
tomorrow *n.* ashita, asu 明日
tonight *n.* komban 今晩
too *adv.* (also) ...mo ...も ...mo mata ...も又 (overly) ammari あんまり
tooth *n.* ha 歯
toothbrush haburashi 歯ブラシ
toothpaste hamigaki 歯磨
toothpick tsumayōji 爪楊枝
top *n.* itadaki (mountain) いただき teppen てっぺん
total *n.* zembu 全部 gōkei 合計 *adj.* zentai no 全体の
touch *vt.* sawaru さわる fureru 触れる
tough *adj.* (thing) katai 堅い (healthy person) jōbu na 丈夫な (patient person) nebari-zuyoi ねばり強い (work) tsurai つらい
tour *n.* ryokō 旅行
tourist *n.* kankōkyaku 観光客
toward *prep.* ...no hō e ...の方へ
towel *n.* taoru タオル
tower *n.* tawā タワー tō 塔
town *n.* machi 町
toy *n.* omocha おもちゃ
trade *n.* bōeki 貿易
   foreign trade gaikoku bōeki 外国貿易
tradition *n.* dentō 伝統
tragedy *n.* higeki 悲劇
train *n.* (transportation) kisha 汽車 densha 電車
transistor *n.* tranjisutā トランジスター
translate *vt.* honyaku suru 翻訳する
travel *n.* ryokō 旅行 *vi.* ryokō suru 旅行する
tray *n.* (o-)bon （お）盆

treat *vt.* (to food) gochisō suru 御馳走する (medically) chiryō suru 治療する

tree *n.* ki 木

trip *n.* ryokō 旅行

trouble *n.* (inconvenience) mendō 面倒 tesū 手数 kurō 苦労 (difficulty) konnan 困難 *vt.* tesū o kakeru 手数をかける

trousers *n.* zubon ズボン

truck *n.* torakku トラック

true *adj.* hontō no 本当の

truly *adv.* hontō ni 本当に

trust *vt.* shinjiru 信じる

try *vt.* kokoromiru 試みる yattemiru やってみる tsutomeru 努める

Tuesday *n.* Ka-yōbi 火曜日

turn *vi.* mawaru 回る *vt.* mawasu 回す

turn on (gas, light) tsukeru つける (radio) kakeru かける (water) dasu 出す

turn off (gas, light) kesu 消す (radio) tomeru 止める

twelve *n.* jū-ni 十二

twenty *n.* ni-jū 二十

twice *adv.* (two times) ni-do 二度 ni-kai 二回 (double) ni-bai 二倍

two *n.* ni 二 futatsu 二つ

typewriter *n.* taipuraitā タイプライター

typhoon *n.* taifū 台風

U

umbrella *n.* kasa 傘

uncle *n.* oji 伯父 (elder than parent) 叔父 (younger than parent)

uncomfortable *adj.* kokochi no yoku nai 心地のよくない fuyukai na 不愉快な

under *prep.* ...no shita ni ...の下に

understand *vt.* wakaru 分る

underwear *n.* shitagi 下着

uneasiness *n.* fuan 不安 **feel uneasy** fuan ni omou 不安に思う

uniform *n.* (costume) seifuku 制服

university *n.* daigaku 大学

unless *conj.* ...nakereba ...なければ

until *prep. conj.* ...made ...迄

unusual *adj.* kawatta 変った

up *prep.* ...no ue ni ...の上に **up to** ...made ...迄

upset *vt.* dainashi ni suru 台なしにする mecha-kucha ni suru めちゃくちゃにする (stomach upset, etc.) guai ga warui 具合が悪い

upside down *adv.* sakasama ni さかさまに abekobe ni あべこべに

urge *vt.* susumeru 勧める

urgently *adv.* kyū ni 急に

use *vt.* tsukau 使う

useful *adj.* benri na 便利な yaku ni tatsu 役に立つ

usual *adj.* futsū no 普通の

V

vacant *adj.* aite iru 空いている

vacation *n.* yasumi 休み kyūka 休暇

vague *adj.* aimai na あいまいな bakuzen to 漠然と

vagueness *n.* aimai あいまい bakuzen 漠然

valid *adj.* yūkō no 有効の

valuable *adj.* taisetsu na 大切な kichō na 貴重な

value *n.* neuchi 値打 kachi 価値

variety *n*. henka 変化 (sort) shurui 種類

various *adj*. iroiro no 色々の chigatta 違った

vegetables *n*. yasai 野菜

very *adv*. taihen 大変 totemo とても hijō ni 非常に

view *n*. (scenery) keshiki 景色 miharashi 見晴し (opinion) iken 意見 kangae 考え

village *n*. mura 村

vinegar *n*. (o-)su (お)酢

virtue *n*. toku 徳

visit *vt*. (a place) otozureru 訪れる (person) tazuneru 尋ねる ukagau (humble) 伺う

vocabulary *n*. kotoba 言葉 goi 語彙

vogue *n*. hayari はやり ryūkō 流行

voice *n*. koe 声

W

waist *n*. koshi 腰

wait *vt*. matsu 待つ (at table) o-kyūji suru お給仕する

waiter, waitress kyūji 給仕

waiting room machiaishitsu 待合室

wake up *vi*. mega sameru 目が覚める okiru 起きる okosu 起す

walk *vi*. aruku 歩く
　go for a walk sampo suru 散歩する

wall *n*. (of house) kabe 壁 (around yard, garden) hei 垪

wallet *n*. saifu 財布

want *vt*. hoshii 欲しい

war *n*. sensō 戦争

warm *adj*. atatakai 暖い

wash *vt*. arau 洗う (laundry) sentaku suru 洗濯する

waste *vt*. muda ni suru 無駄にする

wastebasket kamikuzu-kago 紙屑かご

watch *n*. tokei 時計

water *n*. mizu 水
　waterproof bosui 防水

way *n*. (road) michi 道 (direction) hōkō 方向 (method) yarikata やり方 hōhō 方法
　on the way to chū de 途中で
　way out deguchi 出口

we *pron*. (us) watakushi-tachi 私達 watashi-tachi 私達

weak *adj*. yowai 弱い

wealthy *adj*. yūfuku na 裕福な

wear *vt*. (clothes) kiru 着る (footwear) haku 穿く (headwear) kaburu 被る (handwear) hameru はめる

weather *n*. tenki 天気

Wednesday *n*. Sui-yōbi 水曜日

week *n*. shū 週

weight *n*. mekata 目方

well *int*. de wa では ja じゃ sate さて tokoro de ところで *adv*. (good) yoku よく

west *n*. nishi 西

wet *adj*. nureta 濡れた

what *adj*. nani 何

when *adv*. itsu いつ *conj*. ...... toki ni ...時に

where *adv*. doko どこ dochira どちら

whether ...ka dō ka ...かどうか

which *adj*. dore どれ dochira どちら

while *conj*. ...no aida ...の間

white *adj*. shiroi 白い

who *pron*. dare 誰 donata どなた

whole *adj*. zentai no 全体の subete no すべての

whose *pron.* dare no 誰の donata no どなたの

why *adv.* naze なぜ dōshite どうして

wide *adj.* hiroi 広い

width *n.* haba 幅

wife *n.* tsuma 妻
  my wife kanai 家内

wind *n.* kaze 風
  It is windy kaze ga fukimasu 風が吹きます

wind *vt.* maku 捲く

window *n.* mado 窓

winter *n.* fuyu 冬

wipe *vt.* fuku 拭く

wise *adj.* kashikoi 賢い rikō na 利口な

with *prep.* ...to ...と to issho ni ...と一緒に

without *prep.* (excluding) ...no hoka ni ...の外に (not having) ...nashi ni ...なしに

woman *n.* onna 女

wonder *vt.* fushigi ni omou 不思議に思う

wonderful *adj.* subarashii すばらしい suteki na すてきな

wood-block print *n.* mokuhanga 木版画

wooden clogs *n.* geta 下駄

word *n.* kotoba 言葉

work *n.* shigoto 仕事 *vi.* shigoto o suru 仕事をする hataraku 働く

world *n.* sekai 世界

worry *n.* shimpai 心配 *vi.* shimpai suru 心配する

worse *adj.* motto warui もっと悪い ...yori warui ...より悪い

worst *adj.* ichiban warui 一番悪い goku warui ごく悪い

worth *n.* neuchi 値打 kachi 価値

wound *n.* kega 怪我

wrap *vt.* tsutsumu 包む

write *vt. vi.* kaku 書く

wrong *adj.* (not good) warui 悪い yoku nai よくない (mistaken) machigatta 間違った (reverse) gyaku no 逆の abekobe no あべこべの

Y

yard *n.* niwa 庭

year *n.* toshi 年
  this year kotoshi 今年
  last year kyonen 去年

yellow *adj.* kiiroi 黄色い *n.* kiiro 黄色

yen *n.* en (Japanese money) 円

yes *int.* hai はい ē ええ

yesterday *n.* kinō, sakujitsu 昨日

yet *adv.* mada まだ koremade ni これまでに mō もう

you *pron.* anata あなた, 貴方

young *adj.* wakai 若い

your (yours) anata no あなたの

youth *n.* seinen 青年

Notes